This Work
Dedicated
to the
Christ

THE JOY BOOK

THE WAY OF UNCONDITIONAL LOVE

*A simple way to create
Joy, Prosperity and Unconditional Love
in your life now*

by

Prem Raja Baba

Published by

Prem Raja Baba
Post Office Box 1401
Mount Shasta, California 96067-1401

Second Revision

First Printing: March 1994
Second Printing: March 1996
Third Prnting: July 1998

ISBN 0-9645010-0-7

"In love and service to the planet Earth"

THE JOY BOOK

The way of
UNCONDITIONAL LOVE

TABLE OF CONTENTS

	Testimonials	vi
	Preface	ix
	Introduction	xiii
Chapter 1	The Way It Is	1
Chapter 2	Command Subconscious Programs	12
Chapter 3	Five Steps of Unconditional Love	43
Chapter 4	The Basics of Unconditional Love	54
Chapter 5	Step 1: Circular Connected Breathing	62
Chapter 6	Step 2: Complete Relaxation	77
Chapter 7	Step 3: Awareness in Detail	83
Chapter 8	Step 4: Integration into Ecstasy	90
Chapter 9	Step 5: Do It Now! Be Spontaneous	99
Chapter 10	Morning Kickstart	109
Chapter 11	Integrating Pain	111
Chapter 12	Integrating Illness	116
Chapter 13	Commands for Love, Liberation and Ascension	121
Chapter 14	Putting It All Together	129
	Readers Want to Know	132
	Support Services	137

TESTIMONIALS

"There are not enough words to express my profound and utter delight, the almost instant effect on me and my life, the first day of reading and putting to use your suggestions. Within hours I felt I could fly. Chronic fatigue, I have had for years was gone, bright happy outlook and a magnificent sense of peace...came over me, is still with me. My God am I grateful for this wonderful work . I LOVE IT! It works! I love the simplicity of it all and you are correct, it is the most important book I will ever read."

Linda Glassburn

"When this book was brought to my attention I knew it was a book sent to me from God. I'm sure it will help me achieve the next highest vibration and consciousness level of awareness. My thanks to Prem Raja Baba for his contribution and sharing of this information."

Gloria J. Parker, Publisher, Aquarius Magazine

"The subconscious programs have assisted me immensely. I use them daily for healing myself physically and emotionally. I have used your work to assist hundreds of people with wonderful results. Thank you for your leading edge technology and your service to the world."

Sally Moon
TV and radio talk show host
Metaphysical teacher/Personal Growth Consultant

"Several Months ago I discovered lumps in my breasts (there was a lot of soreness). So I used both the HEALTHY BREASTS and the CANCER FREE PROGRAMS. The lumps and the soreness were gone within two days. Thank you so much for your wonderful programs......I have been taking quinine sulfate for foot and leg cramps. Using Prem's method (synthesis of drugs), I synthesized the quinine into my body. Within minutes the cramp was gone."

G. Martin

"I have recently spent some quality time with Prem Raja Baba and I have learned some powerful techniques that I know I will use for a long time to come. Prem's integration techniques have helped me almost instantly turn a negative mental state into a positive one.

In particular, I have found that I can direct my subconscious to bring me into a state of joy and ecstasy in the midst of circumstances that once caused great upset or conflict. So, instead of writing out long sets of affirmations or having to stop what I am doing to deep breathe or meditate for an hour, I find I can `get off it' very quickly now.

The Command Subconscious Programs are great. I have found the `Slim Down' program to be very effective. I am losing weight steadily without dieting. The weight loss is slow, but permanent."

Rose Kelly
Professional Rebirther
Reiki Therapist

"For nineteen years I have had problems and infections with my urinary tract system that required me to constantly be on antibiotics. After using the Command Subconscious Programs and doing the drug synthesis process, I have not had any further problems. Several times I have awakened with a headache, sore throat or neck pain. After using the Command Subconscious Programs the pain was gone within five to fifteen minutes. After I did the ADDICTION FREE PROGRAM I stopped drinking coffee immediately. My health has improved dramatically since I began using this technology. The Command Subconscious Programs have been a miracle in my life and I am very grateful for them. Thank you!

Karin Stenius

I have used all the technologies in this book for many years and they have brought me great joy and empowerment. The friends and students I have shared them with have experienced extraordianary transformations and miracles. I am totally alive and empowered due to these teachings and I love it. My life is effortless.

There is rarely a week that goes by without someone calling or writing me about how excited they are with this book and how it is changing their lives. The Joy Book is fast becoming a best seller by "word of mouth." I feel so blessed that this book has assisted so many in healing, transforming and empowering and it excites me to think of how many millions of lives will be transformed by this simple little book.

Prem Raja Baba
Author and publisher of The Joy Book

PREFACE

It is a time of Ascension for all: you, me, other starseeds and the planet herself. Before Ascension can be fully embraced, we must be prepared. We must purify our bodies: our light bodies, physical bodies and most of all our mental and emotional bodies.

Over the years I have met many who believe that purifying the physical body is most important. What I have found is that if the mental and emotional bodies are purified, the physical will automatically become pure. I am not saying to eat garbage. I am saying that the focus must be on the mental and emotional bodies first and foremost.

All toxins and poisons being held in the physical body are reflections of thoughts, fears, beliefs and emotions that are being held in the mental and emotional bodies. Clearing these thoughts, fears, beliefs and emotions out of the mental and emotional bodies will automatically release the toxins and poisons from the physical body.

The technology in this book is designed to prepare everyone for ascension by purifying the mental, emotional and physical bodies. The programs in chapter two are designed to purify the mental body which will make purification of the emotional and physical bodies easier than any other method. The five steps of unconditional love will bring you fully into your heart which is important since the heart is the eighth chakra, the Ascension chakra.

There are other new techniques in the book that will make you more autonomous and even save you hundreds of dollars a year in vitamins, minerals, nutritional supplements, drugs and medicines. Everything you require is to be manifested by a mere command. There is no further need for rituals. The more you practice the techniques in this book the closer you will come to full empowerment and full ascension.

Some of it is new technology and you may not have a paradigm for it all. Reread it a few times. Where it says to memorize the five steps, it is important to memorize them and it is only a few words anyway. Highlight the important statements or the ones that you don't fully understand. Go back and reread them later. Keep a pad and pencil close by and take notes.

Don't compare this technology to anything else you are familiar with. Let go of old ideas and beliefs. You must close the doors to the old ways in order to open the doors to this technology. Many try to put this in a paradigm where it won't fit, something like trying to watch a color television program on a black and white television set. It just won't work the way it is suppose to.

This is not really a book. I know I call it a book and it may look like one and is even found on a book shelf in a book store, but it is actually a transformational system. Once you begin reading this book the book will begin reading you. Part of the system is a total restructuring of your consciousness to fit this new technology. Allow it to happen. The book is a vehicle in which God is able to work through most efficiently. Only ten percent of what you get from this book is through reading. Ninety per cent comes from God.

Many have defined Ascension as returning to our ships or being rescued from the planet by being beamed up to a starship by the Ashtar Command. Ascension as I have experienced it is being in the moment totally. Being in power totally. This means not giving your power away to anyone or anything or any event. This is the power of manifestation, happiness, joy and love. It is all there unconditionally. What humans have been led to believe is that in order to manifest anything, one must do or give something in return, to be conditional. Ascension is being a lily in the field. Just being and not doing! We are human beings, not human doings. All we are and have is from God.

Why go through a middleman when we have the power to go straight to the source? This book and the technology within it is all the knowledge you require to go direct to the source unconditionally. It is all you require for your empowerment and Ascension. Don't get discouraged. You may experience learning plateaus and this is normal. Spirit is working with you even now in preparing you for the next page. Surrender to spirit and let God take you to your Ascension. Begin now!

INTRODUCTION

Think for a moment what it would be like to be a member of a primitive tribe. You haven't even invented the wheel and horses are used only for food. Travel is only by foot. It is slow and laborious at best. If you are in a hurry, you can sprint at twenty to twenty-five miles per hour at great effort.

Your tribes people have never seen any modern devices and don't even have a paradigm for the wheel. One day a twentieth century explorer comes upon your tribe. He is driving a four wheel drive automobile across the flats at high speed. What do you do?

Probably, your first response would be to doubt your senses. Question whether what you are seeing is real or a dream. You haven't ever seen anything like it, not even a primitive horse drawn wagon. You have no paradigm for it. There is no thought structure or experiences that comes close to being able to support or explain what you are seeing. As it approaches, you go into fear. What is it? What does it want? Instead of welcoming a new technology and experience into your life, you run and hide.

From within this frightening device emerges a human. Both of you have lived on the same planet since birth yet this modern being seems totally alien to you. You think maybe he came from another planet or is a God or something. The unknown answers to your pressing questions panics you. Do you run or confront your worst fears? Are you willing to overcome your primitive fears and embrace a new day and a new way or are you choosing to let it pass you by?

I know there is something to be said about being primitive and simple, but this is not about that. It is an analogy to assist you in understanding and preparing yourself for the technology in this book. It is highly advanced and most have no paradigm for it. Like the four wheel drive automobile, you don't have to understand how it works, but just that it does work and how to use it.

Getting back to the story, you now have the choice of being the first in your tribe to experience this new technology or you can run in fear and do it later or not at all. Progress is inevitable. Why not surrender to it? Here is a technology that will make travel almost effortless for your tribe. Similarly, the technology in this book can make transformation quick and almost effortless for you and your tribe, family, friends and clients.

You can create your own ending to this story and how you are. The same can be said about this book. There are many responses. One could be of total overwhelm. For some it will be like going from high school science to quantum physics. For some it is the next step and they are ready. If this book doesn't come easy at first, don't give up. It is easier than you think. It may just be subconscious fear that is blocking your ability to comprehend and absorb. Subconscious fear is fear that we are unaware of yet it effects our life and well being.

The reaction of the primitive was fear. This book can evoke fear of the unknown just as that automobile does to a primitive native. Remember that the primitive native was afraid of something that is very common in our society. We would think it laughable to be afraid of an automobile and someday this book and its technology will be as common place as the automobile or the telephone.

When Marconi, the inventor of the wireless radio told his friends and family that he could communicate without wires, they thought he went mad and had him committed to a mental hospital. Only after demonstrating his new invention did they see the light. They had no paradigm for his technology.

You must allow a paradigm to be created within your consciousness so that you have a place to put the information from this book. For some, this will mean reading the book a piece at a time and pausing for a period of time. For others, it may mean reading the book two or three times.

To make it easier to absorb and understand this technology you may want to do the following techniques.

Take the book and hold it to your heart with both hands and say: "Align and absorb, appropriate time elapses". Your subconscious will scan and read the whole book, making it easier for you to understand, absorb and comprehend it.

Another way to assist you is to put this book under your pillow every night while you sleep.

Whatever way you choose to integrate this book and its technologies into your life, remember that it is easy and that it is not IQ that makes it easier to understand but the presence of a paradigm.

If you have questions, please write me with them and send a self addressed and stamped envelope for the response. My address is on the title page of this book. I welcome all comments and questions. There are no stupid questions, only stupid answers.

This may well be the most important book you will ever read.

CHAPTER ONE

The Way It Is

It has been said that the only way to enter the kingdom of Heaven is as a little child. As strange as it may sound, this is true. When one is as a child is, one is in pure joy. Most of us have had this experience and lost it early in life. If you are willing, you can rekindle that heavenly experience of joy and unconditional love and integrate it into your every moment and experience.

For most, joy was lost early in childhood. It was then that our parents (and the rest of society), not knowing better, taught us CONDITIONAL LOVE through judgment. It was their method of controlling us, rewarding us when we were good or right and punishing us when we were wrong or bad. From this continuous judgmental reward/punishment experience we learned what our parents (and society) believed to be right and good and wrong and bad. These models were induced into our minds and somewhere around the age of eight or so years we began to use this false knowledge to run our own lives.

Just as if we were carrying our parents, teachers, ministers, and guardians around with us in our subconscious minds, we began judging ourselves (and others) and creating our own punishments and rewards. Judgment feeds our desires to please our parents and others. It has become a driving force that has created suffering and lack for most people. It could be the root cause of all suffering and lack on the planet. If nothing else, it has robbed you of the joy and unconditional love you deserve now.

THE JUDGMENTAL MECHANISM

Besides being a conscious habit that we use daily (rewarding and condemning all we see), this learned judgment has became a subconscious mechanism that has drained us of our heritage of joy. As most people go around judging everything and everyone in their life, they remain unaware of that subconscious judger that is doing the same to them; every judgment bringing either a reward or a punishment.

The kinesthetic feeling we all experience when judged (either by ourselves or by others) is usually one of discomfort (if judged bad) or pleasure (if judged good). This feeling is energy within our bodies. It is energy in motion or E-motion. All conscious judgment results in immediate E-motional experiences. Subconscious judgment occurs in the average person at close to the speed of light. Since we allow ourselves to be aware of only one fraction of all our subconscious thoughts, only the emotions of a fraction of all our judgment are experienced kinesthetically. All the other judgmental results are held in storage as thought energy.

This thought energy is stored around the physical body, usually in locations associated with what was judged. If not released or experienced, this thought energy becomes additive, building upon itself until the local cells cannot tolerate the intensity of the energy. It is at this time when one becomes aware of this energy in the form of aches and pains, or illness and organ dysfunction. Remedies such as aspirin, antacids, acupuncture, rolfing, massage, spiritual healing, etc. are Band-Aids. They treat the symptoms but not the true cause. The true cause of all illness and human suffering is Judgment and the thought energy it produces.

THE POWER OF THOUGHT

Thought is creative. This is the only absolute law in the universe. All other laws, we as humans, either singularly or in mass, created as an act of God. Karma is one of these laws and will be discussed more fully later in the book. Since thought is creative then we as thinkers are creators. This means our life experience is the sum total of all our thoughts at this very moment. How we look, how we feel, the people we are with, the money we have, our health, our happiness or misery are all a reflection of our thoughts. The totality of all our thoughts is something no one person can comprehend for it includes the subconscious as well as the conscious mind. Research psychologists say that our minds produce somewhere around fifty thousand thoughts a day. If we consider the subconscious, the number may be more like fifty million. Each one of these thoughts produces a result in our lives that we personally experience.

If a large percentage of a persons thoughts are produced by the judgmental mechanism, it would be safe to say that ones life might be an experience of self punishment, with a few rewards thrown in for good judgments. This judger can be equated as carrying around our parents with us. Imagine the punishments they would impose upon us for things we have done or have thought (yes, our judger judges us for our thoughts as well as our actions) and look at our life and see if some of those same punishments haven't manifested at one time or another.

When people are upset or feel guilty, they sometimes lose their appetites and can't eat; not unlike being sent to bed without their dinner. People who enjoy being spanked during love making might have unresolved guilt feelings about sex. Loneliness could very well be a punishment like being sent to our room when we were a child. Even work can be seen as a punishment if when, as a child, we were punished by being given chores and work while everyone else played. Loss of money or valued possessions might be equated to having our allowance or toys taken away by our parents.

The judger is a complex mechanism and may operate in numerous different ways in each individual, but these ways are fundamentally the same in design. The differences are the models it uses (to compare with) and how punishments and rewards are created.

The judger or judgmental mechanism within all of us works very much like the judicial system in our society. And why not? Our government is just a reflection of our consciousness in mass and is reflecting that judger within all of us. Most citizens don't have any awareness of the thousands of defendants that are processed through our legal system daily and it is a reflection of the thousands of judgment made by our subconscious judger that we also are unaware of.

THE JUDGMENTAL SPIRAL
What is created in our lives is what is called the JUDGMENTAL SPIRAL. Remember that the judger is working all the time comparing every thought and act with models previously placed in our minds. So, as we think or do something,

our judger compares it with whatever is in the model file within our mind that closely fits it. If what we are doing or thinking matches the model and the model is labeled GOOD, we are judged as DOING GOOD and might even create a reward for ourselves. If it matches a model labeled BAD, we will be judged as bad or GUILTY and create our own punishment.

THE JUDGMENTAL SPIRAL

Examining the good judgment for a moment, the result or reward might be experienced as feeling very high, euphoric, lucky, having a good day, receiving gifts, money or love.

As for the results of a judgment of guilt, a series of events follow as does a judgment in a court of law. The punishment may be experienced as feeling depressed, suffering a loss, becoming ill, being attacked physically or sexually, having an auto accident, divorce, and death (either by natural or unnatural causes) and more.

The way the judgmental spiral works is that judgment brings guilt. Then there is a request for punishment (sentencing). As with the court procedures, sentencing can be carried out immediately after judgment or may be delayed for quite some time as with capital punishment.

A delay of punishment means that the subconscious is sending out a request to the universe for punishment and it hasn't occurred yet. The way the subconscious transmits this request is by mental telepathy.

Most of our communications are non-verbal and mental telepathy is one of the nonverbal methods we use. The conscious reaction is an experience of fear. This fear manifests in the form of phobias (fear of flying, fear of heights, fear of the water, etc.), allergies, hives, or overt aggressive defensive actions (anger, hostility). Since overt expressions of anger is not acceptable in our society, our judger deems us guilty again and the circle becomes a spiral as it becomes additive and intensifies.

Mood swings or bi-polar manic depressive disorders may very well be caused by the judger within. If all rewards are given at one time, the person would swing into euphoria or a great high. Then when punishment is dealt, depression is experienced. As I said before, each judgmental mechanism works differently and that may be why only certain people experience manic depression.

Is paranoia, a mental disorder characterized by delusions of persecution, also a result of the judger within? Intense guilt may cause a subconscious (telepathic) request for punishment in a nonspecific form. Subconsciously the person has knowledge of this request and what surfaces is a fear that almost every person is a possible executioner. Something like having a KICK ME sign pasted on our back.

DOVETAILING

Now that it is clearer that we are responsible for creating all our experiences, even what we deem the bad ones, it may be possible for us to accept the fact that there are no victims. All aggression and violence is created by all parties involved. The so called victims subconsciously judge themselves and then request punishment. The so called criminal is an aggressor looking for a place to happen. The two attract each other to satiate their needs. Just like two sides of a drawer are joined together with a dovetail joint, fitting perfectly, so does the so called victim and criminal dovetail perfectly.

Judgment and guilt aren't the only causes of dovetailing for all our needs and desires are fulfilled by others that fit our needs and desires. All gifts are from those willing to give. Even a thief is just someone receiving a gift, for what was stolen was given subconsciously by the victim. Emotional attraction may be just the subconscious alignment of two peoples' needs and desires. And when the desires are complete or their needs fulfilled, they may repel each other and separate.

KARMA

There may be a correlation between what was judged and the type of punishment created. If we believe in the "AN EYE FOR AN EYE, A TOOTH FOR A TOOTH" concept, this will hold true. What we do to others will come back to us.

"What goes around comes around". Some people call it "THE LAW OF KARMA". In reality it is the law of our own sub-conscious judicial system working overtime. If we steal, we will be robbed. If we inflict pain, we will experience pain. If we abandoned someone, we will be abandoned and so on. It is refreshing to note that the law of Karma can be wiped from our law books now once it is understood. It isn't necessary to punish ourselves for things we did in the past or even in past lives anymore. We are and have always been innocent because there are no victims. Whatever was done to others, was requested or commanded on some level of our consciousness.

For those who have experienced Intense incidents such as rape, murder, war, holocausts, it is difficult to understand all the elements that went into is creation. The enormous pain and suffering that they had to endure is a memory lodged deep in their soul. I had an intense personal experience that had almost destroyed me. It took ten years to recover from it. The hatred and rage I had for those who hurt me was overwhelming. It was only when I realized that somewhere within my own consciousness I had co-created the event. My guilt produced requests for self punishment coupled with my intentions as a Christ being here to liberate the planet from darkness (when you challenge evil, it will counterattack) was enough to manifest hell on Earth. I deprogrammed the judgment, invoked protection and integrated the rage and forgave them and myself.

Crib deaths, deformed infants, retardation, abortions, and any death or affliction at an early age are usually caused by past life judgment where the sentence (punishment) hadn't been carried out before death. In these instances the being carries the past life judgment into its next life for execution of punishment. This, of course is totally unnecessary. It is important to note that we as humans do make mistakes. Judging our actions only creates more problems, more complexities, and more difficulties.

Holocausts, where thousands die may have been caused by group or mass consciousness requesting punishment. The miracle child or person dug out of the rubble or wreckage alive and unscathed is just one not requesting death as a punishment. People whose religions are based much on sin and guilt seem to create disasters. South America is overrun with disaster (wars, earthquakes, etc.) and the population is primarily Catholic. Those who suffered the most in the Ethiopian drought were the Jews and the Catholics. There seems to be a correlation between guilt based religions and societies and their experiencing of holocausts and disasters.

Death in all forms may be punishment requested, not just by accident or murder but even old age or aging itself. For thousands of years there has been a quest for the secret of eternal youth, the secret that would stop aging. One contributing factor that causes aging is the simple belief that we are born, we grow old and we die. Remember that a belief is a thought and thoughts create. How fast we age, and when and how we die may resemble how our parents aged and died for much of our beliefs come from them. Other factors causing the aging process is guilt and suppressed rage. Aging is no more than continuous death on the cellular level of our bodies. As life continues, so does the death request until an organ fails, total body dysfunction occurs, or one creates forgiveness and lives forever. Death urge or death request with rage is what causes death. Rage is a killing energy and is necessary before anyone can kill themselves, others or even a fly.

Death and illness are sometimes blamed on microorganisms called virus and bacteria and they truly do cause it. What has to be understood is our relationship to these organisms and our responsibility for the death and illness. As with any request for punishment, it isn't necessary for another human to be the executioner. We execute many of our own punishments and also request execution from microorganisms. Even though we can't see them, there are trillions of virus and bacteria in the air and on everything we touch. The reason everyone isn't ill is because we all don't request illness as punishment. Sickly people may be guilt ridden beings requesting punishment from local bacteria. Remember that thought is creative and we can be as creative as we like in producing our life experiences. The use of microorganisms to serve us is just one way.

THE BRIGHTER SIDE

Well, now for the uplifting news: Since thought is creative and we as thinkers are creators, the only barrier stopping us from receiving everything we want is our thought structures in the form of our limiting beliefs and worthiness level (which is controlled by our subconscious judger). As our judger pronounces judgment minute by minute we may become worth less and less. As our worthiness level lowers, it becomes more difficult to get what we want. We have to work harder to receive and sometimes we lose what we have already gained. So, to experience abundance, all that is required is to forgive ourselves, to know that we are and have always been innocent, to modify our judgmental mechanism to reflect our innocence and to let go of all conscious and subconscious limiting beliefs.

Environmental modification is important. When listening to the average person one usually hears contrary thoughts expressed. This verbage (verbal garbage) is a product of the personal judicial system and a reflection of limiting beliefs. Statements as routine as: "It's a miserable day", "I hate the rain", "He's no good at all", "it tastes bad", It will never work", "I can't", are sample reflections of what society as a mass consciousness is thinking. Exposure to this rampant judgment and limiting beliefs only reinforces what one wants to discard. For this reason it is very important that we avoid contrary, limiting and judgmental environments and surround ourselves as much as possible with people who are willing to support us in being non-judgmental, unlimited and powerful.

It is also important to free ourselves from our own limiting beliefs and judgmental system that resides in our subconscious. Years ago, I would have recommended affirmations or mantras. Since then, I have discovered a new and highly effective system of reprogramming the subconscious that has brought about great transformations and healings in the lives of those that have used it. Affirmations are okay, but if you were to compare affirmations to this new system, it would be like comparing the covered wagon to the space shuttle. This new system is called Command Subconscious Programs.

Since the first printing of this book, it has been discovered that as starseeds, our intentions to liberate this planet has attracted evil beings to us that cause us problems. They use our contrary thoughts and suppressed emotions against us and are able to add to them. So, besides thought, actions and intentions can also create. Someday, maybe soon, evil will be a thing of the past.

CHAPTER TWO

Command Subconscious Programs

This new technology has been named COMMAND SUB-CONSCIOUS PROGRAMS. Why command? Because these programs assist us in effecting command of our life experience by reprogramming our subconscious.

Your subconscious mind does everything for you. You are basically the ship commander. All muscle coordination, all actions (walking, running, thinking, seeing, tasting, talking) are done by your subconscious. You just command your subconscious to do it. How well your subconscious performs depends on how well it was trained or programmed. How well you perform and experience life is up to you and how you command and program your subconscious.

If certain experiences in your life are not what you want, experiences like lack, struggle, illness, loneliness, or pain to name a few, it is time to reprogram your subconscious and tell it just what you want. Sometimes it is as simple as telling your subconscious what result you desire and other times it takes reprogramming. Since most of what you do was taught to your subconscious by others (parents, teachers, ministers,

TV and mass consciousness) your subconscious does most of what it does to their specifications and not yours. You are living your life to other's beliefs and not your own. You are the captain of your ship and your subconscious is your crew. Do you want your crew doing things your way or the way other captains do it? Do you want your parents, teachers and ministers to rule your life through past programming or do you want to take command of your life now?

HOW THIS SYSTEM WORKS

This chapter has a list of programs that will effect transformation of your life experience, heal illnesses, and increase your abilities. By following the step-by-step instructions, you can telepathically retrieve any or all of the programs listed in this chapter and use them to transform your life. There are also techniques in the back of the chapter that will assist you in creating a more effortless life for yourself.

Probably the best way to explain these programs is to see our minds as personal computers. If we want to change the way our computers operate, we just change the software. The software that may have served you earlier in life may not be beneficial to you now. Just as you would erase the old software programming and install the new programming, the CSP's do the same. Once a program is requested, your memory and consciousness is totally scanned and a program is custom created for you and is written in your soul language. This program is designed to restructure your system so that you can get the results you desire. It is then installed in your consciousness telepathically by God. Once installed, the Command Subconscious Programs run automatically and continuously and are updated by God daily.

13

How quickly you will experience results from these programs is dependent on many factors. Basically, if you have been wearing glasses for thirty years, it may take awhile to rewrite your consciousness. If a problem or illness has been with you for a short time, results will be quicker.

For addiction programs, you must take action. The program will remove the addiction, but you must take the initiative and stop doing the habit. Halting drug use or smoking with these programs is easy and there will be no withdrawal pains, but you must stop using the drugs or smoking, the programs will do the rest.

Healers can use these programs with their clients to augment their own healing gifts and techniques. Follow the same directions as for giving programs to children. Since the client has given permission for you to heal them, these programs can be given with or without their knowledge. I suggest that healers do acknowledge the programs to their clients. Remember to do what is for the highest benefit of them.

CONNECTING WITH YOUR SUBCONSCIOUS
The first step is to personify your subconscious. This creates an easy way for you to communicate with that what seems intangible. Give your subconscious a name and a gender. Make it your first officer or executive secretary. This is not a major decision. If you come up with a different name in the future, just change it. The same goes for the gender. I recommend people use their middle name if they like it.

Telepathy from the subconscious can sometimes be blocked by evil beings. Telepathy from the higher self cannot. To guarantee retrieval of your programs, do the same for your higher self as you just did for your subconscious. When retrieving your programs, choose either your subconscious, your higher self or both to make telepathic contact with God.

TAKE COMMAND

Once you have made contact with your subconscious, you have now opened up a command channel that allows you to choose your life experiences. Besides the CSP's, just talking to your subconscious before doing anything can improve the results. Just tell your subconscious what you want to experience. Tell it what results you want. Before rolling the ball down the alley, a bowler would tell its subconscious that it wants to knock down all the pins with one ball. Just before it is thrown to him, a wide receiver would tell its subconscious it wants to catch the ball and run at top speed to the TD zone unimpaired. A young woman making love might tell her subconscious that she wants multi-orgasms and not to become pregnant or contract any diseases. Your subconscious is at your service. Tell it what you want. There are functional commands in the back of the book that will assist you greatly.

REPROGRAMMING THE SUBCONSCIOUS

Sometimes telling our subconscious what we want is not enough. For most of us, our subconscious has been programmed with contrary and limited beliefs that hamper us in getting what we want effortlessly. Up until now, reprogramming was done mostly by doing affirmations, a long and tedious method that didn't always guarantee results. Command Subconscious Programs is a method of reprogramming the subconscious that is highly effective and effortless. Comparing affirmations to the programs in this book is like comparing a covered wagon to the space shuttle.

Since Command Subconscious Programs put you in command of your body and life experience, the name is quite appropriate. CSP's are available through this book. I, Prem Raja Baba have been blessed with the ability to create CSP's and have been telepathically giving them to people for quite some time. This book is a simple system has been created for everyone to retrieve these programs. I have found that some have a trust issue with telepathy. For this reason, you can now request these programs directly from God. This book shows you effortlessly how to telepathically communicate with God and retrieve your programs.

The way the CSP's work is simple. You choose a problem you want to solve, an illness you want to heal, or a specific goal you want to obtain. Look up the program in this book under either the goal you want to achieve or the illness/problem you are experiencing. Ask your subconscious to retrieve the chosen program by following the simple instructions. Once installed, the programs run automatically and continuously and are updated daily by God.

Once God has a request to create a program for you, your whole consciousness is scanned for thought structures that are creating your problem/illness or keeping you from your goal. From that information, a program is created using future technologies, paradigms beyond human comprehension and it is installed in your subconscious. One part of the program is designed to dissolve the contrary thought structures and integrate any energies associated with them. The other part of the program creates new thought structures to create your desired experience. This all takes place in less than a minute and CSP's can be created for one or a million people at the same time.

Even though these programs are very effective in changing life experiences and consciousness, they are not always to be relied upon exclusively. If you are currently taking action to solve a problem or heal yourself, continue taking that action. Use the CSP's to augment those actions. For some goals, the CSP's are quite effective on their own and others require holistic techniques.

RETRIEVING PROGRAMS

Before choosing and retrieving programs from the lists, first retrieve the EMPOWERMENT PROGRAM, the SAFE PROGRAM, and the JOY PROGRAM. These programs are foundation programs. Using these programs make the other programs so much more effective as well as making your life easier and more enjoyable.

HERE IS A DESCRIPTION OF THESE PROGRAMS:

EMPOWERMENT PROGRAM: This program is designed to align your subconscious and conscious minds so that they are rowing in the same direction. After doing this program you will find life to be much easier and much less of a struggle.

SAFE PROGRAM: This program updates your EGO defense system by redefining what is truly dangerous and what is safe and pleasurable.

JOY PROGRAM: This program moves your life experience from one of fear and survival into one of joy, peace and love.

FOLLOW THESE SIMPLE INSTRUCTIONS

1. CHOOSE A NAME AND GENDER FOR YOUR SUBCONSCIOUS. You can use your middle name, or any name

that pops into your awareness. If desired, these choices can be changed at any time.

2. ASK YOUR SUBCONSCIOUS BY NAME TO RE-TRIEVE YOUR PROGRAM. Just fill in the blanks below with your <u>subconscious's name</u> and the <u>name of the selected program</u> and say the following to yourself:

(<u>subconscious name</u>), PLEASE MAKE TELEPATHIC CONTACT WITH GOD AND RETRIEVE MY (<u>name of program</u>) PROGRAM NOW.

For the three foundation programs, retrieve them by saying the following:

(<u>subconscious name</u>), PLEASE MAKE TELEPATHIC CONTACT WITH GOD AND RETRIEVE MY EMPOW-ERMENT PROGRAM NOW.

(<u>subconscious name</u>), PLEASE MAKE TELEPATHIC CONTACT WITH GOD AND RETRIEVE MY SAFE PROGRAM NOW.

(<u>subconscious name</u>), PLEASE MAKE TELEPATHIC CONTACT WITH GOD AND RETRIEVE MY JOY PRO-GRAM NOW.

Once you have retrieved your CSP's, they automatically run continuously and are updated daily by God to maintain them at peak effectivity.. While retrieving the programs, focus on your body and you may feel a change or shift in your energy as the programs do their work. Some experience the energy shift and some don't, so don't be concerned if you don't. The programs are still working.

CHOOSING AND RETRIEVING
PROGRAMS FROM THE LISTS

THE FOLLOWING ARE SAMPLES

Say you are experiencing a headache. Look through the ILL-NESS/PROBLEM LIST left column for HEADACHE. Once you have found HEADACHE, look to the right of it and you will see the name of the program you will retrieve. The name of this program is HAPPY HEAD. Ask your subconscious to retrieve the HAPPY HEAD PROGRAM by saying the following:

(subconscious name), PLEASE MAKE TELEPATHIC CONTACT WITH GOD AND RETRIEVE MY HAPPY HEAD PROGRAM NOW.

Say you want to increase your prosperity. Look through the GOAL PROGRAMS LIST left column for PROSPERITY. Once you have found PROSPERITY, look to the right of it and you will see the name of the program you will retrieve. In this case the name of this program is PROSPERITY.

Ask your subconscious to retrieve the PROSPERITY PROGRAM by saying the following:
(subconscious name), PLEASE MAKE TELEPATHIC CONTACT WITH GOD AND RETRIEVE MY PROSPER-ITY PROGRAM NOW.

You may notice that many of the programs for the different ailments and problems have the same names. If you require two different programs that have the same name, the program will become a compound program, that is, both programs integrate into one and run together on command.

SPECIAL INSTRUCTIONS FOR
GOAL ORIENTED PROGRAMS

For programs that will create a specific desired result, you must choose specifically what that result is to be. Once you have your specifications in your mind, then retrieve your program. It is recommended that you write these specifications down on paper for reference later, even though this is not required.

For weight loss or gain, choose a target weight. For breast enlargement or reduction, choose a breast size and chest size. If you desire a lover or friends, be specific and in detail when formulating how those people are to be. Include physical features as well as mannerisms and how they will respond to you. You may also include wealth, health, common interests, etc.

ABORTION AND BIRTH CONTROL

This book is not intended to take any position either fore or against abortion or birth control. I have left it up to God. When you retrieve the abortion or birth control program from God, it will work if God has intended for you to have that experience. If it doesn't work, then God has intended for you not to have that experience. I recommend that you be surrendered to whatever experience occurs. That way it is purely God's decision.

EMOTIONS

Since most illnesses and problems are a manifestation of suppressed emotions, it is recommended that you search within your self for the emotions you are holding and express them in a healthy manner. This will assist in your healings and transformations. The CSP's are not to be used to avoid experiencing your emotions. If an ailment that you are healing is caused by suppressed or repressed emotions, the program will assist you in bringing those emotions up so that they can be expressed or integrated in a healthy manner. Once the emotions have surfaced, use the Five Steps of Unconditional Love to joyfully integrate them.

If you have anger or rage, take a bat and beat on a bale of hay or anything that is soft. If you have grief, find a safe and quiet place and cry as long as you have to. For some, crying may be intense and lengthy. This is okay and beneficial. These emotions are energies held within you. They must be expressed or they manifest as illness, pain and struggle. Let go of any belief or judgment you may have about expressing emotions. Know that the expression of all emotions is healthy and natural. To get into your emotions, get out of your head (thoughts) and into your heart.

FOR YOUNG CHILDREN (AND CLIENTS)
Since young children cannot read or follow these simple instructions, the parents can choose to do the following.

1. Choose the programs that you want your child to have (Always include the EMPOWERMENT, JOY and SAFE programs).

2. Say the following to retrieve each program for your child. It will be sent to your child's subconscious telepathically.
(your subconscious name), PLEASE MAKE TELEPATHIC CONTACT WITH GOD TO GIVE (your child's name) his/her (name of program) PROGRAM NOW.

For example, if I want my son to get A's in school effortlessly, I would say the following:

RAJA, PLEASE MAKE TELEPATHIC CONTACT WITH GOD TO GIVE JASON HIS SCHOLASTIC ACHIEVEMENT PROGRAM NOW.

RAJA is the name of my subconscious, JASON is my son's name, and SCHOLASTIC ACHIEVEMENT is the name of the program that will assist him in getting straight A's in school. Do this method with any of the programs.

This same method can be used with those unable to do it on their own as well as clients of healing professionals, and even those in comas. Verbal permission is a prerequisite but if this is not possible, just retrieve the programs for the person anyway. God will make telepathic contact with the person and ask permission. When permission is given, the programs will go in. Clients of healing professionals give you permission when they ask you to assist them in healing.

Some people are dedicated to evil and will block any assistance from the Christ. They won't get the programs. Dedication, contracts and possession of evil can happen to anyone. It's quite common. Doing the following commands/invocations will usually clear this problem. I recommend you do them daily.

I UNDEDICATE MYSELF FROM EVIL AND DEDICATE MYSELF TO THE CHRIST!

I CANCEL ALL CONTRACTS BETWEEN MYSELF AND ALL EVIL!

GOD, DEPOSSESS ME NOW!

REVIEW

This technology is all new to the world. Because we don't have a paradigm for this technology, it may be necessary for you to read the instructions at least three times to fully understand them. All you are doing when you use these programs is retrieving a custom designed program written in your soul language that will rewrite your consciousness so that it is in alignment with what you want in life now. You only have to retrieve each program ONCE. That installs it in your consciousness and runs it continuously. To maintain their effectiveness, all programs are updated by God daily.

If you don't find the program you are looking for in the list of programs, create your own. Simply set the goals of the program in your mind and give it a pleasant name. Once this is done, simply retrieve it as you would any other program.

Again, the simple steps are as follows:

1. GIVE YOUR SUBCONSCIOUS A NAME AND A GENDER

2. ASK YOUR SUBCONSCIOUS TO RETRIEVE YOUR PROGRAMS

3. YOU ONLY NEED TO RETRIEVE EACH PROGRAM ONCE

4. SINCE THE CAUSE OF AN AILMENT MAY VARY FROM TIME TO TIME, RETRIEVE A NEW PROGRAM EACH TIME AN AILMENT REOCCURS TO INSURE THE PROGRAM IS ADDRESSING THE CAUSE OF THAT AILMENT.

SIMPLIFICATION

Because this book is the physical aspect of an enormously powerful healing system, the system can change and the processes in this book will always be valid.

Since the first printing of this book, how the Command Subconscious Programs are retrieved has been streamlined. Now, instead of having your subconscious make telepathic contact with God, you can retrieve Command Subconscious Programs by just saying: "GOD, GIVE ME MY (name of program) COMMAND SUBCONSCIOUS PROGRAM NOW."

TO RETRIEVE A PROGRAM FOR YOURSELF

GOD, GIVE ME MY (name of program) COMMAND SUBCONSCIOUS PROGRAM NOW.

TO RETRIEVE A PROGRAM FOR SOMEONE ELSE

GOD, GIVE (name of person) HIS/HER (name of program) COMMAND SUBCONSCIOUS PROGRAM NOW.

It is this simple. Nothing else to do. Retrieve your programs, live your life and practice loving yourself unconditionally.

GOAL PROGRAMS LIST

GOAL/DESCRIPTION	PROGRAM NAME
ABUNDANCE, material and financial	ABUNDANCE
ASCENSION, higher spiritual consciousness	ASCENSION
ASSISTANCE from others	TOTAL ASSISTANCE
ASTRAL TRAVEL	ASTRAL
ATHLETIC ACHIEVEMENTS, exceeding limits	GOLD MEDALIST
AWAKE AND ALERT, stay alert while driving	ALERT
BEAUTIFUL HAIR	BEAUTIFUL HAIR
BEAUTIFUL SKIN	BEAUTIFUL SKIN
BIRTH EFFORTLESSLY & pleasurably	JOYFUL BIRTH
BIRTH CONTROL, temporary sterility	STERILE
BIRTH CONTROL, temporary fertility	CONCEPTION
BODY PURIFICATION, detoxification	PURE BODY
CHAKRAS, open fully	CHAKRAS
CLAIRAUDIENCE	CLAIRAUDIENCE
CLAIRVOYANCE	CLAIRVOYANCE
COURAGE, getting or having more	COURAGE
CREATIVITY	CREATIVITY
DIVORCE, joyful marriage completion	GREAT DIVORCE
DNA CHANGE, to 12 light encoding filaments	DNA
EMOTIONAL PURIFICATION	EMOTIONS
EMPLOYMENT	GREAT POSITION/JOB
ENLIGHTENMENT, high spiritual goal	ENLIGHTENMENT
FEARLESSNESS	FEARLESS
FERTILITY	FERTILITY
FINANCIAL PROSPERITY,	FINANCIAL PROSPERITY
FORGIVENESS	FORGIVENESS
FREEDOM	FREEDOM
GRIEVING, releasing suppressed grief	GRIEVING
GROUNDING	GROUNDING
HAIR GROWTH, eliminate baldness	HAIRY HEAD
HEALTHY BODY, maintain a healthy body	HEALTHY BODY
HIGH IQ	GENIUS
HIGH SELF ESTEEM	SELF ESTEEM
INDEPENDENCE	INDEPENDENCE
INTIMATE RELATIONSHIP, create a lover	LOVERS AND FRIENDS
JOY, for your subconscious	INNER JOY
LIGHT BODY, increase your spiritual light	LIGHT BODY
MANTRAS, mantras done thousands of times	MANTRAS
MEDITATION, improves meditation	MEDITATION
MEMORY IMPROVEMENT	MEMORY
MOSQUITO REPELLENT, psychic mosquito shield	MOSQUITO SHIELD
MUSCLE POWER, increase	POWERHOUSE
PATIENCE	PATIENCE
PHYSICAL IMMORTALITY	PHYSICAL IMMORTALITY
PLEASURE, creating more in your life	PLEASURE
PROSPERITY, unlimited flow of money/material	PROSPERITY
PSYCHIC ABILITIES	PSYCHIC
REBIRTHING, assists one in the process of rebirthing	REBIRTHING

GOAL/DESCRIPTION	PROGRAM NAME
RECEIVING, increase your ability to	JOYOUS RECEIVER
RELATIONSHIP COMPLETION	JOYOUS GOOD-BYES
RELATIONSHIPS, friends	ABUNDANT FRIENDS
RELATIONSHIPS, lovers	WONDERFUL LOVERS
RELEASING THE PAST	JOYOUS RELEASING
SCHOLASTIC ACHIEVEMENT, getting A's easily	SCHOLASTIC ACHIEVEMENT
FIVE STEPS, maintains you in the 5 steps	FIVE STEPS
SUCCESS OF A COMPANY	COMPANY SUCCESS
SUCCESS IN A PROFESSION	PROFESSIONAL SUCCESS
TELEPATHY	TELEPATHY
UNCONDITIONAL LOVE	AGAPE
WEIGHT GAIN(choose a target weight)	WEIGHT GAIN
WEIGHT LOSS(choose a target weight)	SLIM DOWN
WHOLENESS, total integrity	WHOLENESS
YOUTHING, rejuvenating your body	YOUTHING

Understand that there are many factors involved in reprogramming your subconscious. These factors may effect the results you get from the above programs. Usually results are experienced in days or weeks. If your apposing thought structure is massive, that will lengthen the time it takes before you experience results. Usually results are obtained within one year. Sometimes, it is not spiritually beneficial for you to obtain a goal. In that case there will not be any results from that program until your spiritual goals change.

If you are possessed by an evil entity, devoted in any way to evil or have contracts with evil, they may be keeping you from your desired experiences. Do the commands/invocations on page 22 to clear yourself. There may also be times when evil beings will block your telepathy preventing retrieval of your Command Subconscious Programs. If you sense this occuring, give your higher self a name and gender and command your higher self to make telepathic contact with God and retrieve your Command Subconscious Programs using the same format you used with your subconscious. I know that some people don't believe in evil. I recommend you do these anyway. It couldn't hurt!

ILLNESS/PROBLEM LIST

ILLNESS/PROBLEM	PROGRAM NAME
ABDOMINAL CRAMPS	HAPPY TUMMY
ABSCESS	ABSCESS FREE
ABUSE	RESPECT & NURTURE
ACHES	PLEASURE
ACNE	BEAUTIFUL SKIN
ADDICTIONS	ADDICTION FREE
ADDISON'S DISEASE	HEALTHY ADRENALS
ADENOID PROBLEMS	HEALTHY ADENOIDS
ADRENAL PROBLEMS	HEALTHY ADRENALS
AIDS	HIV FREE
ALCOHOLISM	ALCOHOL FREE
ALLERGIES	ALLERGY FREE
ALZHEIMER'S DISEASE	HEALTHY NERVOUS SYSTEM
AMENORRHEA	HEALTHY WOMAN
AMNESIA	FULL MEMORY
DYSENTERY	AMOEBA FREE
ANAL ABSCESS	HEALTHY ANUS
ANAL FISTULA	HEALTHY ANUS
ANAL ITCHING	HEALTHY ANUS
ANEMIA	RED BLOOD
ANKLE PROBLEMS	HEALTHY ANKLE
ANORECTAL BLEEDING	HEALTHY ANUS
ANOREXIA	PERFECT BODY
ANXIETY	TOTALLY SECURE
APATHY	TOTAL JOY
APPENDICITIS	HEALTHY APPENDIX
ARM PROBLEMS	HEALTHY ARM
ARTERIOSCLEROSIS	HEALTHY ARTERIES
ARTERY PROBLEMS	HEALTHY ARTERIES
ARTHRITIS	HEALTHY JOINTS
ASTHMA	FREE BREATHING
ASTIGMATISM	20/20 EYESIGHT
ATHLETE'S FOOT	HEALTHY FEET
BACILLARY DYSENTERY	BACILLARY FREE
BACK PROBLEMS	HEALTHY BACK
BAD BREATH	SWEET BREATH
BALDNESS	HAIRY HEAD
BEDWETTING	DRY SLEEP
BLADDER PROBLEMS	HEALTHY BLADDER
BLEEDING GUMS	HEALTHY GUMS
BLISTERS	HEALTHY SKIN
BLOOD PRESSURE PROBLEMS	HEALTHY BLOOD PRESSURE
BLOOD PROBLEMS	HEALTHY BLOOD
BODY ODOR	FLOWER BODY
BOILS	HEALTHY SKIN
BONE MARROW PROBLEMS	HEALTHY BONE
BONE PROBLEMS	HEALTHY BONES

ILLNESS/PROBLEM	PROGRAM NAME
BOWEL PROBLEMS	HEALTHY BOWELS
BRAIN TUMOR	TUMOR FREE
BREAST PROBLEMS	HEALTHY BREASTS
BRONCHITIS	HEALTHY LUNGS
BULIMIA	GENTLE APPETITE
BUNIONS	HEALTHY TOES
BURSITIS	HEALTHY BURSA
CANCER	CANCER FREE
CANDIDA	CANDIDA FREE
CANKER SORES	HEALTHY MOUTH
CARTILAGE OF THE KNEE	HEALTHY CARTILAGE
CATARACTS	HEALTHY EYES
CELLULITE	SMOOTH SKIN
CEREBRAL PALSY	HEALTHY BRAIN
CHOLESTEROL HIGH	LOW CHOLESTEROL
CODEPENDENCY	INDEPENDENCE
COLD	HEALTHY BODY
COLIC	COLIC FREE BABY
COLITIS	HEALTHY COLON
CONGESTION	HEALTHY LUNGS
CONJUNCTIVITIS	HEALTHY CONJUNCTIVA
CONSTIPATION	HEALTHY BOWELS
CORNS	HEALTHY FEET
CORONARY THROMBOSIS	CLEAR ARTERIES
COUGHS	COUGH FREE
CRAMPS	SAFE AND RELAXED
CROSSED EYES	HEALTHY EYES
CROUP	HEALTHY RESPIRATION
CYSTIC FIBROSIS	HEALTHY GLANDS
CYSTITIS	HEALTHY BLADDER
CYSTS	CYST FREE
DEAFNESS	HEALTHY HEARING
DEMENTIA	TOTALLY SANE
DEPRESSION	JOY-ELATION
DIABETES	HEALTHY PANCREAS
DIARRHEA	HEALTHY COLON
DIGESTION PROBLEMS	HEALTHY DIGESTION
DIZZINESS	STABILITY
DRUG ADDICTION	DRUG FREE
EAR PROBLEMS	HEALTHY EARS
EMPHYSEMA	HEALTHY LUNGS
ENDOMETRIOSIS	HEALTHY WOMAN
EPILEPSY	HEALTHY NERVOUS SYSTEM
EPSTEIN-BARR VIRUS	VIRUS FREE
EXOTROPIA	SELF APPROVAL
ECZEMA	HEALTHY SKIN
EYE PROBLEMS	HEALTHY EYES
FACE PROBLEMS	HEALTHY FACE
FAINTING	TOTALLY CONSCIOUS
FATIGUE & CHRONIC FATIGUE SYNDROME	ALIVENESS
FEET PROBLEMS	HEALTHY FEET

ILLNESS/PROBLEM	PROGRAM NAME
FEVER	98.6 DEGREES
FEVER BLISTERS	HEALTHY LIPS
FINGER PROBLEMS	HEALTHY FINGERS
FISTULA	I AM SAFE
FLATULENCE	HEALTHY DIGESTION
FLU	HEALTHY BODY
FRIGIDITY	SEXUAL PLEASURE
FUNGUS PROBLEMS	FUNGUS FREE
GALL BLADDER PROBLEMS	HEALTHY GALL BLADDER
GALLSTONES	HEALTHY GALL BLADDER
GANGRENE	HEALTHY TISSUE
GAS PAINS	GAS FREE
GASTRITIS	GAS FREE
GENITAL PROBLEMS	HEALTHY GENITALS
GLANDULAR FEVER	HEALTHY GLANDS
GLANDULAR PROBLEMS	HEALTHY GLANDS
GLAUCOMA	HEALTHY EYES
GOITER	HEALTHY THYROID
GONORRHEA	GONORRHEA FREE
GOUT	GOUT FREE
GRAY HAIR	YOUNG HAIR
GINGIVITIS, GUM PROBLEMS	HEALTHY GUMS
HALITOSIS	SWEET BREATH
HAND PROBLEMS	HEALTHY HANDS
HAY FEVER	ALLERGY FREE
HEADACHE	HAPPY HEAD
HEARING PROBLEMS	LOUD AND CLEAR
HEART PROBLEMS	HEALTHY HEART
HEARTBURN	HEALTHY TUMMY
HEMORRHOIDS	HEALTHY ANUS
HEPATITIS	HEALTHY LIVER
HERNIA	HERNIA FREE
HERPES I	HERPES FREE
HERPES II	HERPES FREE
HIP PROBLEMS	HEALTHY HIPS
HIVES	HEALTHY SKIN
HODGKIN'S DISEASE	HEALTHY BODY
HUNTINGTON'S DISEASE	HEALTHY NERVOUS SYSTEM
HYPERACTIVITY	TOTALLY RELAXED
HYPERGLYCEMIA	HEALTHY PANCREAS
HYPEROPIA	20/20 EYESIGHT
HYPERTENSION	TOTAL RELAXATION
HYPERTHYROID	HEALTHY THYROID
HYPOGLYCEMIA	HEALTHY PANCREAS
HYPOTHYROID	HEALTHY THYROID
IMPOTENCE	HEALTHY SEX
INDIGESTION	HEALTHY DIGESTION
INFECTION	INFECTION FREE
INFLAMMATION	INFLAMMATION FREE
INFLUENZA	INFLUENZA FREE
INSANITY	TOTAL SANITY

ILLNESS/PROBLEM	PROGRAM NAME
INSOMNIA	RESTFUL SLEEP
INTESTINAL PROBLEMS	HEALTHY INTESTINES
ITCHING	HEALTHY SKIN
JAUNDICE	HEALTHY LIVER
JAW PROBLEMS	HEALTHY JAW
ILLNESS/PROBLEM	PROGRAM NAME
JOINT PROBLEMS	HEALTHY JOINTS
KERATITIS	HEALTHY EYES
KIDNEY PROBLEMS	HEALTHY KIDNEYS
KIDNEY STONES	HEALTHY KIDNEY
KNEE PROBLEMS	HEALTHY KNEE
LARYNGITIS	HEALTHY LARYNX
LEG PROBLEMS	HEALTHY LEGS
LEPROSY	LEPROSY FREE
LEUKEMIA	HEALTHY BLOOD
LEUKORRHEA	HEALTHY WOMAN
LIVER PROBLEMS	HEALTHY LIVER
LOCKJAW	TETANUS FREE
LOU GEHRIG'S DISEASE	HEALTHY BODY
LUNG PROBLEMS	HEALTHY LUNGS
LUPUS	HEALTHY SKIN
LYMPH PROBLEMS	HEALTHY LYMPH SYSTEM
MALARIA	MALARIA FREE
MANIC DEPRESSION	PEACE AND JOY
MASTITIS	HEALTHY BREASTS
MASTOIDITIS	HEALTHY MASTOID
MENOPAUSE, stop or delay	YOUNG WOMAN
MENSTRUAL PROBLEMS	JOYFUL WOMAN
MENTAL ILLNESS	PEACE AND JOY
MISCARRIAGE PROBLEMS	HEALTHY FETUS
MONONUCLEOSIS	MONO FREE
MOUTH PROBLEMS	HEALTHY MOUTH
MUCUS COLON	HEALTHY COLON
MULTIPLE SCLEROSIS	HEALTHY NERVOUS SYSTEM
MYOCARDIAL INFARCTION	HEALTHY HEART & LUNGS
MYOPIA	20/20 EYESIGHT
NAIL BITING	PEACE AND JOY
NAIL PROBLEMS	HEALTHY NAILS
NAUSEA	HEALTHY APPETITE
NECK PROBLEMS	HEALTHY NECK
NEPHRITIS	HEALTHY KIDNEY
NERVOUS BREAKDOWN	PEACE AND JOY
NERVOUSNESS	TOTAL RELAXATION
NEURALGIA	PAIN FREE
NOSE BLEEDS	HEALTHY NOSE
NOSE PROBLEMS	HEALTHY NOSE
NOSE STUFFED	FREE BREATHING
NUMBNESS	TOTAL FEELINGS
OSTEOMYELITIS	HEALTHY BONES
OSTEOPOROSIS	HEALTHY BONES
OVARIAN CYSTS	HEALTHY OVARIES
OVARY PROBLEMS	HEALTHY OVARIES

ILLNESS/PROBLEM	PROGRAM NAME
OVERWEIGHT	SLIM DOWN
PAGET'S DISEASE	HEALTHY BODY
PAIN	PLEASURE
PALSY	HEALTHY BODY
PANCREAS PROBLEMS	HEALTHY PANCREAS
PANCREATITIS	HEALTHY PANCREAS
PARALYSIS	TOTALLY ANIMATE
PARASITES	PARASITE FREE
PARKINSON'S DISEASE	HEALTHY BODY
PEPTIC ULCER	HEALTHY DIGESTIVE SYSTEM
PERIODONTITIS	HEALTHY GUMS
PETITE MAL	NO MAL
PHLEBITIS	HEALTHY VEINS
PILES	HEALTHY RECTUM
PIMPLES	HEALTHY SKIN
PITUITARY PROBLEMS	HEALTHY PITUITARY
PLANTAR WART	WART FREE
PNEUMONIA	HEALTHY LUNGS
POISON IVY	HEALTHY SKIN
POISON OAK	HEALTHY SKIN
POLIO	HEALTHY BODY
POST-NASAL DRIP	HEALTHY SINUSES
PREMENSTRUAL SYNDROME	JOYFUL WOMAN
PROSTATE PROBLEMS	HEALTHY PROSTATE
PRURITUS	HEALTHY SKIN
PSORIASIS	HEALTHY SKIN
PYORRHEA	HEALTHY GUMS
RABIES	RABIES FREE
RASH	HEALTHY SKIN
RECTUM PROBLEMS	HEALTHY RECTUM
RHEUMATISM	HEALTHY BODY
RHEUMATOID ARTHRITIS	HEALTHY JOINTS
RICKETS	HEALTHY BONES
RINGWORM	WORM FREE
SCABIES	SCABIES FREE
SCIATICA	HEALTHY NERVE CELLS
SCLERODERMA	HEALTHY SKIN
SCOLIOSIS	HEALTHY SPINE
SEIZURES	SEIZURE FREE
SHINGLES	HEALTHY SKIN
SICKLE CELL ANEMIA	HEALTHY BLOOD
SINUS PROBLEMS	HEALTHY SINUSES
SKIN PROBLEMS	HEALTHY SKIN
SMOKING	TOBACCO FREE
SORE THROAT	HEALTHY THROAT
SORES	HEALTHY SKIN
SPASMS	SPASM FREE
SPASTIC COLITIS	HEALTHY COLON
SPINAL MENINGITIS	HEALTHY SPINE
SPINE PROBLEMS	HEALTHY SPINE
SPLEEN PROBLEMS	HEALTHY SPLEEN
SPRAINED ANKLE	HEALTHY ANKLE

ILLNESS/PROBLEM	PROGRAM NAME
STERILITY	FERTILITY
STIFF NECK	TOTAL RELAXATION
STIFFNESS	FLEXIBILITY
STOMACH PROBLEMS	HEALTHY STOMACH
STREP THROAT	HEALTHY THROAT
STROKE	HEALTHY BRAIN
ILLNESS/PROBLEM	PROGRAM NAME
STUTTERING	FLOWING SPEECH
STY	HEALTHY EYES
SWELLING	HEALTHY BODY
SYPHILIS	SYPHILIS FREE
TAPEWORM	WORM FREE
TEETH PROBLEMS	HEALTHY TEETH
TESTICLE PROBLEMS	HEALTHY TESTICLES
TETANUS	TETANUS FREE
THROAT PROBLEMS	HEALTHY THROAT
THRUSH	HEALTHY MOUTH
THYMUS PROBLEMS	HEALTHY THYMUS
TICS	TIC FREE
TINNITUS	HEALTHY EARS
TOE PROBLEMS	HEALTHY TOES
TONGUE PROBLEMS	HEALTHY TONGUE
TONSIL PROBLEMS	HEALTHY TONSILS
TUBERCULOSIS	HEALTHY LUNGS
TUMORS	TUMOR FREE
ULCERS	ULCER FREE
URETHRITIS	HEALTHY URETHRA
URINARY BLADDER PROBLEM	HEALTHY URINARY SYSTEM
URINARY INFECTIONS	HEALTHY URINARY SYSTEM
UTERUS PROBLEMS	HEALTHY UTERUS
VAGINITIS	HEALTHY VAGINA
VARICOSE VEINS	HEALTHY VEINS
VENEREAL DISEASE	VD FREE
VIRAL INFECTION	HEALTHY BODY
VULVA PROBLEMS	HEALTHY VULVA
WARTS	WART FREE
WEAK BLADDER	HEALTHY BLADDER
WEAKNESS	STRENGTH
WRIST PROBLEMS	HEALTHY WRISTS
YEAST INFECTION	HEALTHY WOMAN

PROGRAM FORMATS

TO RETRIEVE A PROGRAM
(<u>subconscious name</u>), PLEASE MAKE TELEPATHIC CONTACT WITH GOD AND RETRIEVE MY (<u>name of program</u>) PROGRAM NOW.

OTHER SUBCONSCIOUS POWERS

These programs are only the beginning of a great new technology designed to put you in total command of your life experiences and your body. Below are just a few of the many commands that have been proven effective in changing our life experience for the better. While you are doing these, focus on your body and you will probably feel the shifts in your energies as you say the commands.

INTEGRATION
We all have been programmed to suppress and repress our emotions on a moment to moment basis. These emotions are actually E-Motions or energy in motion that we stop from flowing when we suppress or repress them. The process of getting them flowing and releasing them joyfully is called INTEGRATION. To accomplish this, just say the following:
(subconscious name), PLEASE RELEASE AND INTEGRATE ALL PATTERNS OF ENERGY IN MY BODY INSTANTANEOUSLY AND CONTINUOUSLY.

FULLY OPENING ALL OF YOUR CHAKRAS
When our CHAKRAS or energy centers of the body stay open our life force energy flows effortlessly. To open your CHAKRAS say the following:

(subconscious name), PLEASE OPEN ALL OF MY CHAKRAS FULLY NOW.
Your CHAKRAS will now open to a configuration most beneficial to you.

SOURCING GOD FOR YOUR LOVE

Our love comes direct from God. We need not source it from any person or thing as that is what co-dependency is. When we do source it from a person or thing we tend to shut down our own God source. To reconnect and open your God source of love and light say the following:

(subconscious name), PLEASE CONNECT ME TO MY GOD SOURCE, OPEN IT UP FULLY AND PERMEATE EVERY CELL OF MY BEING WITH GOD'S LOVE AND LIGHT NOW.
This can also be acomplished by saying: GOD, I SOURCE YOU FOR MY LOVE.

MEDITATION

Instead of spending time moving your body into a meditative state, simply command your subconscious to bring you into a deep meditative state by saying the following:
(subconscious name), PLEASE BRING ME INTO A DEEP MEDITATIVE STATE OF CONSCIOUSNESS NOW.

Once your subconscious has brought you into a meditative state, have it integrate all your patterns of energy, open your chakras, and connect you to your God source.

I have a watch with a fifteen minute timer. Every fifteen minutes, I command my subconscious to integrate all of my patterns of energy, to open all of my chakras fully and connect me to my God source fully. It has really made a difference in my life and it only takes a few seconds to do. If fifteen minutes is to frequent, then do it every hour. Besides the primary benefits of this practice, it also gets you used to working with your power and your subconscious and God on a moment to moment basis instead of once in awhile.

SYNTHESIS OF FOOD, DRUGS, VITAMINS, MINERALS, ETC.

During Ascension week 1992 in Mt. Shasta I met a woman who demonstrated the benefits of Takion Beads. I muscle tested stronger with the beads in my hand then without them. Not wanting to pay $84.00 for the beads, I put a few of them in my left hand and commanded my subconscious to scan the takion beads and synthesize them into every cell of my being. It worked! Afterwards, she tested me and there was no difference with or without me holding the beads. You can do this with any substance. Synthesis is a learned process for your subconscious. It may take a few attempts before it works well for you so don't get discouraged with your early results.

SYNTHESIZING FOOD

If you are dieting, fasting, or just feeling hungry and not able to eat at that moment, just tell your subconscious to synthesize food. The hunger will disappear. Just say:
(subconscious name), PLEASE SYNTHESIZE FOOD NOW.

SYNTHESIZING DRUGS

If you require drugs and would like to have their benefit without the side effects or the expense, just put the drug in your left hand and say: (subconscious name), PLEASE SCAN THIS (name of drug) AND SYNTHESIZE IT INTO MY BODY FOR MY HIGHEST BENEFIT. Some of you may not trust this in the beginning, so keep your drugs with you in case you need them. Again, the more you do this the greater the effect. Once you have scanned the drug, you need only command your subconscious to synthesize that particular drug into your body for your highest benefit.

SYNTHESIZING VITAMINS AND MINERALS

You can source light as your 100% source for energy and nourishment and stop eating completely. Your body has the ability to synthesize vitamins, minerals, protein, etc. Just say: (subconscious name), PLEASE CONTINUOUSLY SYNTHESIZE ALL THE VITAMINS AND MINERALS NECESSARY TO MAINTAIN PERFECT HEALTH AND CHEMICAL BALANCE OF MY PHYSICAL BODY.

To Source light, say the following: (subconscious name), PLEASE SOURCE LIGHT AS MY 100% SOURCE OF ENERGY AND NOURISHMENT. This won't happen instantly, but the more you command it the faster the transformation will happen.

ACUPUNCTURE AND ACUPRESSURE

For those of you that are schooled in acupuncture or acupressure, Stimulation of any points on your body or your client's body can be accomplished by your subconscious. Just say: (subconscious name), PLEASE STIMULATE THE FOLLOWING ACUPUNCTURE/ACUPRESSURE POINTS ON MY/HIS/HER BODY FOR ____ MINUTES. (Then list the points).

Another way your subconscious can effect healings on you and others is to tell it to make telepathic command with a specific healing master of the Christ and retrieve all the knowledge necessary to effect a complete healing and then tell it to do the healing. An example of this would be someone that wants the effects of a complete acupuncture treatment now. They would just say: (subconscious name), PLEASE MAKE TELEPATHIC CONTACT WITH AN ACUPUNCTURE (or other healing) MASTER OF THE CHRIST AND RETRIEVE ALL THE KNOWLEDGE NECESSARY TO

FACILITATE A COMPLETE HEALING ON ME (OR WHOMEVER). IDENTIFY AND STIMULATE THE APPROPRIATE ACUPUNCTURE POINTS ON MY (THEIR) BODY FOR TWO HOURS (SPECIFY TIME) TO TOTALLY HEAL (SPECIFY AILMENT). Use this for all healing arts and modalities by adapting it to conform to what you want to happen..

One program that I have named: "THE FRIEND PROGRAM" is a program that uses the telepathic abilities of the subconscious. Actually, all telepathy is through the subconscious. When I ask my subconscious to do "The Friend Program", it makes telepathic contact with the subconscious of every person in close proximity and informs their EGO defense system that I am their friend.

A person's EGO defense system assumes one to be a FOE until identified as a FRIEND. Until identified as a FRIEND, a person tends to keep their distance. When your subconscious does this program, people will respond in an open and very friendly manor towards you. This works for animals also.

Once, I saw a horse being led down the main street. I asked my subconscious to make telepathic contact with the horse and tell it I am its friend. As I approached the horse, it turned towards me and began walking directly to me. When the man leading it pulled on its reigns to guide it straight, it resisted.

To retrieve this program, simply say the following:
(subconscious name), PLEASE MAKE TELEPATHIC CONTACT WITH GOD AND RETRIEVE MY FRIEND PROGRAM NOW.

To use this program, say: (subconscious name), PLEASE DO THE FRIEND PROGRAM NOW.

YOUR SUBCONSCIOUS KNOWS
AND REMEMBERS EVERYTHING

Everyone has misplaced their keys and other objects. This small memory lapse is just a miscommunication between your conscious self and your subconscious. Talk to your subconscious and tell it to give you the location of the lost object.

If you have forgotten a name, address, telephone number, date or other important information, tell your subconscious to search for the specific information and then let go of it. The information will pop into your awareness shortly. The more you do this the less time it will take.

LOVE AND APPROVE OF YOURSELF DAILY

Besides commanding our subconscious to source God as our 100% source of love, it is important to affirm daily our own love for ourselves. Just look at yourself closely in the mirror everyday. I say, "Prem, I love you and approve of you unconditionally now and forever more." Look in your eyes and say: "(your name), I love you and approve of you unconditionally now and forever more."

Do it with your children and loved ones daily saying: "I love you and approve of you unconditionally now and forever more." Getting this into the conscious awareness and energy flows is very important and powerful.

COMMAND THE EXPERIENCE YOU WANT

As said earlier in this book, our subconscious does everything for us. If our personal life experiences are not what we want, it is probably due to old programming that we received from others who didn't know, or from old experiences that we took as the unchangeable truth. Our subconscious was trained to give us certain outcomes from certain scenarios. If we want to change the outcome of any scenario, we only have to tell our subconscious what we want to experience, hence the question: What is the experience you want?

During one of my workshops, a student became fidgety. She shared that it is difficult for her to sit or stay in one place for a long period of time. I asked her: "What is the experience you want? Do you want to be uncomfortable or do you want to be relaxed and enjoy the experience?" She chose the later. "Well," I said, "tell your subconscious what you want. Say to your subconscious by name that the experience you want at this time is to be relaxed and to totally enjoy being here in this workshop." She did that and immediately felt a shift in her energy. This was her first experience of being in command of her life.

This book is designed to empower you. After reading this book, your thoughts will manifest quicker than ever before. I suggest that before you do anything, you state the experience you want from that scenario. If you don't do this, your fears or old beliefs may quickly manifest what you fear or have believed to be the truth in the past. It only takes a few seconds to specify what you want.

This can be done on a daily basis, a general basis and a moment to moment basis. when you awake, tell your subconscious exactly (be very specific) what you want to experience during the day. If you have a schedule or certain events taking place, state how you want to experience them and what your desired outcome is for each event. If you live more spontaneously, tell your subconscious what you want to experience and the outcome you want just before you engage in the event. Some events in our lives repeat on a daily or weekly basis. Relationships, work, school, eating, digesting, eliminating our bowels, playing games, etc. State what you want to experience in these events.

Just like learning to walk, your subconscious may take a little time to retrain itself. For most events, the change will be immediate. There may be some that take a little longer. While playing solitaire one night, I realized that I was losing regularly. I opened up a dialogue with my subconscious and told it that the experience I wanted was to win anytime I played a game. I told it that solitaire was a game. I defined exactly what winning in solitaire was like. Then I resumed playing. I began winning from the first game, but the wins were small. Each time the game was complete, I would tell my subconscious that it was a win, but not the win I wanted. I then repeated the specifications for a win (all fifty-two cards up top.). The wins increased in size until I experienced nine full wins in a row.

Working with God, you can also command your experiences. Just tell God what the experience you want is before it happens. This can be applied to every event in your life. You can do this to specify what kind of day you want, what your money experience is to be, or how you want you love life. Do it for small events like preparing dinner all the way to how you want your whole life to be.

It is important to be very specific when using this command. You can't overdo detail when it comes to this. You might want to write down all specifications before doing this invocation. You can also do this spontaneously from your head. If you change your specifications, just do it again with the new specs. The invocation is as follows:

GOD, THE EXPERIENCE I WANT IS....(specify exactly what you want) and then say: MAKE IT SO!

Here's an example: God, the experience I want is for everyone who reads The Joy Book to transform and ascend effortlessly and joyfully. Make it so! Have fun with it!

CHANGING THE RULES OF THE GAME

Since life is a game, you have the choice of playing it by someone else's rules or making up your own. Living life by someone else's rules is called adapting. I live my life by my own rules and enjoy it. So can you! Create your own rules for your own life that will support you in being the master that you are. Tell these rules to your subconscious and put them in effect now. A few examples are the rules for employees, family members, club members, spiritual people, laws of manifestation, etc.

Changing the rules is just another aspect of telling your subconscious what experience you want. In society, there seems to be an unspoken agreement to go by some rules. As long as you buy into these rules they will rule your life. Make the decision to change the rules that you live by and they will be true for you and others will play by your rules when they are relating to you. You are in power. Take command of your life now!

CHAPTER THREE

The Five Steps Of Unconditional Love

Unconditional love is not something that we read about in verse or talk about in church. Unconditional love is a reality. It is within the reach of all who want it. Most of us were practicing unconditional love when we were born. From that moment on, the mass consciousness of the planet began converting us to conditional love. By the age of eight most of us had lost all vestige of the joy we experienced by loving ourselves unconditionally. We had been trained to love ourselves conditionally.

In order to return to that experience of unconditional love, we must learn how to practice it on a moment to moment basis. The five steps of unconditional love are the elements of unconditional love. The five steps are simple and easy to learn and practice. Since unconditional love is our natural birthright, practicing the five steps is just being naturally who you really are. Since most of us have been practicing conditional love for many years, it may take a bit of practice before unconditional love becomes automatic to you again. It is important to know that practicing the five steps is easy and can be done anywhere and anytime. You can do them while you work or while you play.

THE FIVE STEPS OF UNCONDITIONAL LOVE

Circular Connected Breathing
Complete Relaxation
Awareness In Detail
Integration Into Ecstasy
Do It Now, Be Spontaneous

CIRCULAR CONNECTED BREATHING is the first and chief step. At birth most of us had our umbilical cords cut prematurely before it stopped pulsating. Until the cord stops pulsating, a baby is still relying on the mother for life support. Cutting the cord before a child is fully prepared to breathe on its own puts them in fear of death. Their little computers (minds) takes the experiences and puts them together (fear and not breathing). From this they form their first personal law or belief: <u>When in fear, don't breathe</u>!

This personal law results in most people breathing very shallow, fragmented and holding their breath most of their lives. This is caused by chronic fear, a product of judgment, learned from our parents and society. Now is the time to relearn or unlearn through the practice of full and free breathing all of the time, especially when in fear. As with all the steps, this can only be accomplished through practice.

Doing the Circular Connected Breathing is simple. The inhale is full and positive. At the end of your inhale, immediately begin the exhale. The exhale is to be relaxed and totally uncontrolled. What that means is to just let the exhale fall out. Do not let the exhale out slowly and don't force the exhale out or blow it out. Once the exhale is complete, immediately begin the inhale. Continue this method of breathing until it is automatic.

COMPLETE RELAXATION is the next step and is the opposite of tension. Tension is what we do to suppress and repress (unconscious suppression) emotions. Emotions are energy in motion or E-motions. We learned to suppress certain emotions because we were taught by those around us that expressing them was wrong or bad (judgment). Men shouldn't cry, it isn't lady like to express anger, etc. In some households even laughter had to be suppressed. Tension is the holding of the energy from moving, through the use of an equal and opposite force of energy. Wherever this energy was routed in the body for expression, it is now held there in the form of tension.

When one suppresses crying it causes tension in the sinus area and the lungs which causes headaches, sinusitis, coughs, and what is referred to as the common cold. One needs only to emote to rid themselves of the so called COLD. Suppression of anger causes stiff necks, back problems, shoulder pain and easily injured muscles and backbones. Chronic suppression of E-motions can cause organ failure and illness by overwhelming the cells in that area of the body with excessive energy. This can be equated to exposing the skin (the largest organ in the body) to too much solar energy (sunlight) causing severe burning.

Complete relaxation doesn't come at once but is achieved more and more each day through practice. Complete relaxation is the total lack of the resistance to the flow of energy in the body and one doesn't have to be limp to accomplish it. It is a natural state that will be part of your being whether you are standing, sitting, working, or playing.

When no energy is being used to suppress energy (tension) then more energy is available to accomplish what one wants in life. The point of power is in the present moment. Suppressing energy keeps us in the past or the future. The more the energy from the past and the fear of the future is released the less we are in tension and the more powerful we are to manifest what we want and to live life effortlessly.

AWARENESS IN DETAIL, the third element, is opposite of denial and disassociation. Denial is a practice we learned as a form of self preservation (defense). We learned this when we were very small, either from direct experience or from the experience of one or more of our peers or siblings. Most of us learned it the first time we were punished.

It usually happened by the time we were two years old. We were very small at the time and in comparison, our parents were giants. To really be able to understand the trauma that a child is experiencing when they are that small and being punished put yourself in the child's place. Imagine yourself in a confined room with an eighteen foot tall giant weighing eight hundred pounds, raving mad and screaming that you are wrong or bad and that you are going to "get it". The first thought that will probably enters your mind is: I AM GOING TO DIE. With the giant screaming that the child is wrong or bad immediately creates the personal law: WHENEVER I AM WRONG OR BAD I AM GOING TO DIE. The first action we do in a life threatening situation is to deny and disassociate. That child wasn't allowed its normal reactions of fight or flight. The rage energy that was produced from that frightening experience had to be suppressed. It had to be denied and disassociated for the expression of rage and anger as a child was deemed wrong and punishable, sort of a catch 22 situation created by the parent.

If emotions, thoughts, visions, experiences and feelings are made wrong or bad by our parents and society then anytime we experience being wrong or bad we automatically go into defense posture and deny the thoughts and disassociate the emotions to avoid guilt. Since we are living and experiencing beings we can not go through life without creating these prohibited experiences. Soon we find we have lost much of our awareness. Our bodies have become numb. Many feel dead and seek out drugs such as cocaine to feel alive. Others partake in sports that produce great adrenaline rushes, all to feel that aliveness they lost through denial and disassociation. This is one of the reasons why sex is so popular with its great rush of energy and aliveness and this is also why enlightened beings do not seek out sex with much eagerness for they have the aliveness, awareness and love themselves unconditionally.

Being still is probably one of the best methods of creating awareness. When one is not being distracted by focusing on the outer world, work or play, they automatically start becoming aware of thoughts and feelings they have suppressed; thoughts and feelings they don't want to deal with. To further enhance your awareness, focus on your body as this is where you are storing all you have suppressed in the form of energy.

INTEGRATION INTO ECSTASY is opposite segregation and is the fourth step. Segregation is judgment, comparing black to white and making the black wrong and the white right, the black bad and the white good. Integration is non-judgment. Judgment is comparing what IS to some given model. Since THOUGHT IS CREATIVE and we as thinkers are creators, then all our experiences are a reflection or manifestation of our thoughts and so they are perfect. They can never be wrong or bad and no one is a victim. Everyone's experiences dovetails (fits perfectly) with everyone else's. Once this is understood fully it is easy to see how we are one being moving together in unison or oneness, like members of a symphony orchestra or a dance troupe.

Since conditional love is to love through judgment then unconditional love is to love through integration. When one is in integration, they are in ecstasy. When this occurs on all levels of consciousness, one realizes joy. Since judgment is a habit well learned and practiced by most of society it can be difficult to attain total integration while surrounded by judgmental beings. For those of us willing to work on integration while remaining a member of society it is important to be with others seeking integration and joy. It can be easy to regress when surrounded with judgmental consciousness, so it is important to stay on purpose.

Suppressed E-motions and other patterns of energy may surface to your awareness and cause discomfort or pain. When they do, a simple method of integrating them are as follows. Say: "I AM THIS(THESE) PATTERN(S) OF ENERGY." Also allow the experience to be there. Wanting to get rid of the discomfort is making it wrong and locks it in further.

Remember that anytime you perceive an experience as good, bad, right or wrong you have made a judgment. This should set off an alarm in your head to get back into the fourth step and check the other five steps of unconditional love.

DO IT NOW, BE SPONTANEOUS is number five. All through our lives we seem to seek approval. If you do what others like or think is right or good or try to please others so they will approve and love you, this is conditional love. Our parents and society continuously teach this. As a child we were punished for our spontaneity and so we fear punishment any time we act without judgment.

Being spontaneous is to do whatever you want to without prethought. Prethought is to think before you do. To think whether this will please the person or persons you are with. To think whether they will accept you or like or love you if you do it. We become robotrons acting like everyone else wants us to and not like we want to. We have become performers, always in a role but never being ourselves. It is time to become the spontaneous child again. Watch small children and animals. They are spontaneous. Watch how they are in Joy. Learn from them.

It has been said that the only way to enter the kingdom of heaven is as a little child. A little child is unconditionally loving, spontaneous and creative. If one has to please others for their love then they can not be spontaneous nor can they be creative. They can only act the way people expect them to and nothing more. They have become actors playing the role of the good and right person, acting like others want them to and not being real, alive and honest. Before doing, they always ask is it good or right? Will it please the others? Is it appropriate? If it is not, it is suppressed. People have become robotrons, attempting to please the giant (their parents), and others determined to be a source of love or approval for them. So, the fifth step is to be spontaneous and creative. To let that little child in all of you live in unconditional love. To know that WE are where our love is derived; from US and not externally. We are love.

For those of us that were products of vigorous regimentation as a child, this element may be a challenge. Remembering the thoughts when you were first punished: if I am to live I must please this giant, we can see how scary it can be for some to be spontaneous. I suggest that the easiest way to be in this element is to surround yourself with allowing people and to seek love from your own unconditional source: yourself. It also helps if you allow others to be spontaneous and just do what ever they want and not to judge them. Allow is a very powerful practice; see the perfection in every situation.

This step can also be said to be a culmination of some of the other steps. All our emotions are spontaneous and must be expressed fully and freely when they are created. Do not stifle emotions until an appropriate time, express them when they are created. If you are in the company of non allowing persons, leave and find an area where you can express yourself fully. The best choice is to live and work around people who allow all, unconditionally. If this is possible, do it. But I know for some it is not a choice you have at this time. Don't fret, for it will be a choice soon for thought is creative.

Another part of the fifth step is DO IT NOW. Not only does this mean be spontaneous but to act on your thoughts and desires when you have them. Procrastination is the monkey wrench in the cog works of progress. It walks hand in hand with good intentions in the opposite direction we seek. There is no benefit to any practice or teaching if we are always going to do it later or tomorrow. We must be on purpose and do it now, this very moment, not five minutes from now, or later or tomorrow. Do it now or it probably will never get done.

There is a great resistance in change. This resistance comes from our birth trauma. Birth was our first experience of change and for most it was traumatic. Once bit, twice shy, we shy away from change through procrastination. If we put it off we may never have to change. Even if the change will bring great benefit, we tend to resist change. We must stay aware of this and overcome it by DOING IT NOW.

So, do it now; The five steps of unconditional love. Begin with the first step and once it is learned, go to the next one and on and on and on. Once you have learned the five steps separately, then practice them simultaneously and daily. I recommend that everyone do the five steps every fifteen minutes throughout the day. For some, this may be a bit too much, so for those, do them at least once an hour. You can get wrist watches that beep on the hour to remind you.

In the beginning, it may take a few minutes each time, but after a short while you will find that it only takes a few seconds to check yourself and what you will find is that your experience is one of joy and aliveness.

Since the five steps of unconditional love are a practice that brings one to joy and aliveness, it can be used as a yoga practice. For those on a spiritual quest, the five steps brings great peace when integrated into your daily practices. Do the five steps every morning until you have totally integrated everything activated in the dream state. Whatever you do not integrate from your dream state will create undesirable scenarios during your day that will evoke emotions. This is the way the body integrates patterns of energy when you don't practice the five steps.

Stay conscious of your body as much as possible. When you are experiencing an emotion, be with it. Don't suppress it or make it wrong. Make it fun to express your emotions and it will be fun to express your emotions. Stay in awareness of how you feel and how others feel also. When you feel unalive, it is a sign that you have dropped out of the five steps. Take immediate action and get back in the five steps. Practice makes an athlete a star. As a spiritual athlete, the more one practices the five steps, the faster one achieves their goal of enlightenment, ascension and peace.

Practice and share the Five Steps with your friends and loved ones. The Joy Book was designed to change the world by assisting individuals in changing themselves. As individuals become more joyful and unconditionally loving of themselves, they become a bright light in a not so light world. Their light and love will effect those around them to the point where they will begin to change also.

As an individual, you have the ability to change the world. I invite you to integrate the technology in this book into your life so that you too may assist in the transformation of the planet. Organize your friends and share the teachings of this book with them. Create networks of peace and joy facilitators. Create programs so that you and others can telepathically broadcast affirmations and thoughts of world peace and prosperity continuously each day. Broadcast these affirmations in the first, second and third person. Broadcast affirmations such as: The world is in total peace. Everyone in the world is prosperous and well fed. We are all safe. Use your intuitive sense and your spiritual guidance and TOGETHER WE CAN TRANSFORM THE PLANET.

THE FIVE STEPS OF UNCONDITIONAL LOVE

CIRCULAR CONNECTED BREATHING

COMPLETE RELAXATION

AWARENESS IN DETAIL

INTEGRATION INTO ECSTASY

DO IT NOW, BE SPONTANEOUS

**DO THE FOLLOWING COMMANDS AT LEAST
FOUR TIMES A DAY OR AS REQUIRED**

I undedicate myself from evil and dedicate myself to the Christ!

I cancel all contracts between myself and all evil!

God, depossess me now!

(Do the following before you want to create a desired experience.)

God, the experience I want is......(specify exactly what you want to create).......Make it so! (Use this before everything you do.)

Cut on dotted line and carry with you.

Photocopy this page and place it where you will view it often.

CHAPTER FOUR

Learning The Basics

The five steps is not a philosophy, but a way of life. It was not created to be a topic of discussion, but a practice that one integrates into one's life for the purpose of transforming their life experience to one of joy and ease. In order to facilitate that goal, one has to first learn how to practice the steps, and then to practice them daily. This section of the book is for those who truly want to empower themselves and are willing to devote some time in their lives to becoming who they really want to be now.

The five steps are fairly easy to learn and practice. You will find that the five steps are appropriate to do anywhere, even in the work place. You might want to approach it one step at a time, practicing the first step for a few days or a week until you have championed it. Then move on to the next step. Once the next step is mastered, integrate the practicing of it with the first step. Do the same with the third, fourth and fifth steps.

The Five Steps of
Unconditional Love

CIRCULAR CONNECTED BREATHING
COMPLETE RELAXATION
AWARENESS IN DETAIL
INTEGRATION INTO ECSTASY
DO IT NOW, BE SPONTANEOUS

It is required to commit to memory the five steps to use as a mental checklist, just as the pilot of an airliner knows certain checklists from memory. The easiest way to memorize something is to read it over and over while you are walking or exercising in some manner. When I was a professional actor, I used to roller skate and read my scripts until they were part of me.

You may want to choose an exercise a little safer like a rowing machine or a stationery bicycle. Another way is to write the five steps over and over until you know them. This method is the most common. To make it even easier to memorize the five steps, just think of the acronym **B R A I D**.

Breathing (circular connected)

Relaxation (complete)

Awareness in detail

Integration into ecstasy

Do it now, be spontaneous

However you choose to do it, it is imperative to commit these five steps to memory. Once accomplished, this short checklist will make doing the five steps as simple as 1,2,3......4,5.

Before we begin with the five steps, it is important to review and expand on what was said in part one of this book. The Joy Book addresses and integrates all of what we have taken on from those around us and all the patterns of energy we have suppressed from birth on.

BELIEFS

What people say unconsciously everyday has an effect on those around them. Telepathically, what other people are thinking has an effect on those around them. As we receive these verbal and telepathic messages, we begin to change from the innocent children that we were born as to the struggling and fearful adults we may be now.

As young children, we were non-judging, spontaneous, unconditionally loving, fearless, creative and joyful. Those around us accepted and loved those qualities about us until we reached a certain age when they, for some obscure reason, decided that we must change and be like an adult. Many of us lost some of our child-like qualities earlier due to fearful or rageful parents.

What that meant for most of us was to lose our creativity, our innocence, our spontaneity, our unconditional love, our fearlessness and our freedom. Consider this! Does the reference to adultery in the bible and the ten commandments refer to a violation of marriage vows?

The word adulterate means to corrupt, to debase by the addition of inferior materials. Isn't the true meaning of adultery, before it was changed by religions for their own purposes, really debasing ourselves by the addition of inferior beliefs and thoughts, corrupting ourselves with false fears and limitations?

This form of adultery happens to most of us through our associations with others, with the media, and telepathically through being in mass consciousness.

Two major steps that are recommended are 1. environmental modification and 2. practice the five steps of unconditional love daily. For most, environmental modification means moving away from and breaking ties with those not supporting your being in joy. Again, this book is not to find fault. Those who stand between us and our joy usually genuinely think they are doing what is best for us. We don't have the power or authority to change them, only ourselves. If they cannot accept our transformation and our choices in life, we must separate from them until they see the light.

For some, this may be the temporary cessation of a few friendships or relationships. For others, family ties may have to be broken, temporarily and sometimes even permanently. This may be difficult to understand, but attachments to others usually show a belief that you are not complete and whole on your own and that you need others to experience love. This is just one of those falsehoods we have been given. We must relinquish it, and all other limited beliefs and persons promoting those beliefs from our lives now. For some, that would mean saying good-bye to everyone.

When a ship is taking on water and sinking, bailing the water out will only keep the ship in status quo. The crew will always have to keep bailing the water out until it stops the source of the water from filling up the ship. Once the leaks are patched, the ship can enjoy other endeavors. While the leaks are still there, the crew and the ship remains in survival. Environmental modification is one way to patch up your leaks so you can move on to a better and more joyful life. Once you have created a stabilized experience of joy in your life, you can safely go back to those friends and loved ones and share your joy with them.

For some, environmental modification is not a viable choice. For reasons beyond their control, or due to long term commitments, they must stay with those around them. The five steps will still work for these people; it will just take a little longer. The five steps will be the way that you can stop creating new emotional energies and focus on integrating old suppressed ones.

If you are in an intimate relationship, working together with the five steps will be fun and definitely make it easier. If you are not in an intimate relationship, you might want to do this with a friend. Working in pairs or groups is not necessary, it is just a more effective and fun way of doing them.

PATTERNS OF ENERGY
Throughout the book, we will be mentioning "Patterns of energy". Within our body are many flows of energy. Some flows supply power for our organs and muscles to function. Some are flows of emotions. Some are sensation signals and some, like rage, supply us with the power to fight or run in a dangerous situation.

These are all "Patterns of energy". When they are flowing freely, we experience joy. When these patterns of energy are resisted or stopped from flowing, pain, illness, disease and even death can manifest.

As discussed in the first part of this book, Most of us have learned to suppress one pattern of energy or another. Usually it occurs early in life. Like a savings account, as we suppress more and more of the same type of pattern of energy, it multiplies or compounds with interest.

The most commonly suppressed patterns of energy are: rage, anger, and grief. Many people's reaction to the question of whether they have rage or not is usually an immediate no. When someone denies something immediately, it usually means they are hiding that something. In this case, Rage.

The reason these patterns of energy were and are still suppressed and denied was discussed in the first part of this book. It had to do with the giants (our parents) and how we feared them. Through this fear, we learned, either through direct experience or from our peers, that we must please the giants or die. What this meant was that we must always be good and right, for if we were wrong or bad, we would be punished. And to a little child living with giants, this usually looked like a life threatening situation.

Since the expression of our emotions (even laughing) was sometimes seen as wrong, many have suppressed most of their emotions all of their lives. Rage is usually taught to be wrong and corporally punishable. Anger also is usually not tolerated but some levels of it may have been accepted. Grief, astonishing as it may seem, usually is seen by a parent as a reflection of how good a mother or father they are. Usually knowing very little about being a parent, they unconsciously want to stifle any evidence that would allow their incompetence to be discovered. So, when this type parent sees their child crying, they tend to react by either commanding the child to stop, yelling at the child and making him or her wrong, or by coaxing the child to stop by putting them into denial (telling the child that he/she is okay and that there is nothing to cry about). Either way, the patterns of energy are suppressed and a fear based automatic mechanism is installed in the child's subconscious to suppress all further similar patterns of energy.

Note that these patterns of energy are automatically suppressed by the subconscious because the child was taught to believe, through words, group consciousness and personal experiences that feeling or expressing these emotions or E-motions (energies in motion) would be dangerous, fatal or displeasing to their parents.

Because the expression of some of these E-motions or patterns of energy is seen by our subconscious as dangerous or even fatal, activating them can seem to be very discomforting and frightening for us, even as mature people. The five steps will show you how to integrate these patterns of energy safely, easily and pleasurably. The more of these patterns of energy from your past that you integrate, the more you will be in the present moment, more alive and more in joy.

Suppressed energies hold us in the past. It has been said that, "the point of power is in the present moment". This means that the point of power for you to create and experience life fully is NOW, in this moment. The more fully you are in the present moment, the more intensely pleasurable your immediate life experiences will be. Being completely in the now means letting go of the past completely. The five steps assists you in integrating the past quickly and pleasurably, allowing you to experience and enjoy the present moment fully.

By learning and practicing the five steps of unconditional love you will be clearing your past and maybe even your past lives. You will not only benefit yourself but those around you and the whole planet as well. Before we continue, have you memorized the five steps? If not, it is recommended that you do so now. Once you have the five steps of unconditional love memorized so that you can state them quickly and with little thought, proceed with the first of the five steps.

THE FIVE STEPS OF UNCONDITIONAL LOVE

BREATHING (CIRCULAR AND CONNECTED)
RELAXATION (COMPLETE RELAXATION)
AWARENESS IN DETAIL
INTEGRATION INTO ECSTASY
DO IT NOW, BE SPONTANEOUS

CHAPTER FIVE

Step One
Circular Connected Breathing

Circular connected breathing is simply breathing fully and freely without stopping at the top or bottom of your breaths. Within this method of breathing are three types of breath that can assist you in many ways. The slow and full breath is the standard breath you will use the most. It brings about an experience of relaxation and aliveness. Once you have practiced this breath for awhile, it will become automatic. The other two breaths are special purpose to be used at times of discomfort or illness. These are fast and full and fast and shallow breathing. Combined with the other six steps, these two breaths are very effective in restoring you to an experience of joy quickly and easily.

Before discussing the individual breaths, it is important to know the elements of circular connected breathing. These elements are not anything you don't know how to do now. They are just elements you don't do regularly.

CIRCULAR AND CONNECTED BREATHING

The breath has to be circular and connected. This means that the breath never stops. Once the inhale is complete, the exhale is immediately begun. Once the exhale is complete, the inhale is immediately begun and so on forever. The inhales and exhales don't end abruptly, but taper off. If one was to graph this type of breath, it would look circular in shape and connected in flow.

Most people breathe in a fragmented way. That is, they breathe and stop frequently, the stops being more predominant than the inhales and exhales. Look at how you breathe now. Observe how those around you breathe also. Watching others is a great way of seeing how not to breathe.

RELAXING THE EXHALE

The breath contains energy. As we breath we are taking in and expelling energy from our bodies. The more we breathe, the more energy we have. The more and faster we release our exhale, the easier it is to express and let go of suppressed energies and emotions. People who control their exhale tend to control their emotions. Remember this when you get to step five, DO IT NOW, BE SPONTANEOUS.

So, the idea of a relaxed exhale is not to control the exhale, but to allow it to flow out naturally at its own rate. The easiest way to accomplish this is to focus on your inhale. Let your inhale be positive and strong; masculine in nature. then let the exhale be surrendered, and relaxed; feminine in nature.

One way to describe this breath is to visualize waves breaking on the beach. See yourself as the beach and the waves as your breaths. Your inhale is strong and positive like the waves breaking on the beach. Your exhale is relaxed, and surrendered like the water from the waves returning to the ocean. As soon as the wave finishes breaking, it immediately begins returning to the ocean. No sooner then it has returned then another wave approaches. Breath like the ocean waves now and see how it feels.

Breathe into your lungs and feel them filling. As soon as they are full, immediately relax and allow them to exhale at their own rate. Do this a few times and immediately you will feel more alive. Do it now! Experience a rhythm in your breath. Notice that the inhales take a shorter length of time than the exhales. This is because the exhale is relaxed and uncontrolled.

Remember, do not blow out or hold back the exhale. Also, do not close your jaws and blow through your teeth or whistle the exhale out through your lips. The inhale and exhale should have as little resistance as possible. Keep your mouth open enough to facilitate breathing in and out freely and effortlessly.

CHOOSING AN ORIFICE

Some people like to inhale through their nose and exhale through their mouth or visa versa. You may breathe this way, though I do not recommend it. This switch breathing tends to be distracting and segmenting. It gives the illusion that your breath is circular and connected when in truth, the switching causes the breathing to stop for a microsecond. The breath is truly not circular and connected. For this reason, it is important to choose an orifice and stick with it for awhile. Choose either your nose or your mouth.

For the slow and full breath, you may use either the nose or mouth. For the fast breaths, it is recommended that you use the mouth only. Once you do these breaths, you will see why.

REVIEWING THE BASICS OF BREATHING
Breathe in a circular and connected fashion
Positive inhale coupled with a Relaxed exhale
Choose one orifice and stay with it
Keep the airflow unrestricted
Get into a rhythm

THE THREE BASIC BREATHS
There are four basic breaths that are available to us. They are: SLOW AND FULL, FAST AND FULL, FAST AND SHALLOW and *SLOW AND SHALLOW.* Most people mainly use a segmented slow and shallow breath. This means they breath slowly, only take in a small quantity of air into their lungs on each inhale and pause at the end of each inhale and exhale. This breath is not beneficial and should not be used at anytime.

The other three breaths (fast and full, fast and shallow and slow and full) are really reference points in a spectrum of breathing. The dynamics of your breath will change as required on a moment to moment basis and will not necessarily jump from one extreme to another. The fullness and speed of which you choose to breath will vary within the confines of the definition of each breath.

A slow breath rate can be anywhere from six to fifteen breaths a minute. A fast breath rate can be anywhere in excess of sixty breaths a minute. These are just ballpark figures and may differ with each person. These figures are just for comparison purposes and you should not time your breaths. Similarly, the fullness of your breath may vary also. In full breaths, you may choose to fill your lungs from approximately fifty to one hundred percent of capacity. Remember that as you breath more fully, you will stretch out your diaphragm and your lung capacity will increase.

Once you practice these breaths, you will get an intuitive feeling about them and know just what breath speed and fullness to use. The more you practice these breaths, the easier they are to do and the more comfortable and natural they will feel to you.

SLOW AND FULL BREATHING

When you are tense and in fear, this breath will relax you almost immediately. Use it now and see! First sit back and relax. Now, take three slow full breaths, focusing on the inhales and allowing the exhales to just flow out freely and uncontrolled. Notice the difference in how you feel. Just think how you would feel if you did this breath all day long and not just when you became aware of your tension and fear. You would be relaxed and in joy. When you are relaxed and not in fear and tension, people relate to you better. Your ability to create is increased and you are more in the flow of life itself.

Just for learning purposes I will ask you to time your inhales. Either using the second hand of a clock or the seconds display of a digital watch, take three seconds to fully inhale. Immediately when your lungs are comfortably full, allow the exhale to begin. Notice, I said allow and not start your exhale. The exhale has to be natural and totally uncontrolled. If you were to start it you would be controlling it. So, once you have ended your inhale, just relax your lungs (diaphragm) and let the air flow out freely and uncontrolled. Since your lungs are very much in the center of your body, when you relax them, they tend to effect the rest of the body and it will relax also.

Now that you have an idea as to how to breathe slow and full, practice breathing now for a minute or two. If you get light headed, it is okay. Remember that, at birth, we learned "When in fear, don't breath". The first reaction of slow and full breathing is usually light headedness as it is a reaction of your ego defense system to fear. It is not hyperventilation! It will pass quickly, quicker if you stay relaxed and continue to breath slow and full.

Since this is the first practice of the circular and connected breath, let us review quickly how the breath is done. Beginning with the inhale, breathe in positively, focusing on the inhale. When your lungs are comfortably full, just release the breath and allow the exhale to happen. Just be a witness to the exhale, your body will do the rest. As soon as the exhale is complete, immediately begin the inhale, breathing in positively and fully. Continue this rhythmically. Be aware that the exhales may be longer in duration than the inhales. This is normal and may vary at different times in your life.

It is recommended that you practice this breath for at least one week before attempting to master the fast and full and fast and shallow breaths. Reserve a time in the morning and a time in the evening (thirty minutes to an hour) when you can be quietly alone. Lay down in a comfortable position that is not blocking your nose or mouth, or restricting your throat. Just focus on your breathing. Vary your breath speed and fullness during these sessions to practice control of your breath. Be relaxed and remember to be in the other four steps of unconditional love (Relaxation, Awareness in Detail, Integration into Ecstasy, and Do in now, be spontaneous). You will find the other four steps will come easily and even naturally as you breath and relax.

FAST AND FULL BREATHING
Once you feel you have mastered the slow and full breath, you can go on to learn the two fast breaths. The easiest of these is the fast and full breath. The difference between this breath and the slow and full is the difference between walking and running. Most of us can walk for long periods of time

without getting exhausted, but running is limited by our endurance. The more we practice running, the longer we can run.

Just like running, you may find fast and full breathing exhausting at first. You may not be able to so it for more than fifteen seconds at first. As you practice it, your endurance will improve. One, two or more minutes will be easily obtainable. Since fast and full breathing is only used for short periods, one or two minutes is just fine.

The main purpose of fast and full breathing is to heighten your awareness and aliveness. There are times in our lives when we go into temporary depressions. Symptoms of these depressions are tiredness, boredom, lack of focus and an absence of aliveness and joy. These depressions are usually due to a mass of emotions attempting to surface and your subconscious trying to push them back down. This inner struggle can take much of your energy and put you in a fear/survival mode.

Remember, that if you are not in joy, you are in some level of fear. The way out of fear is by practicing the five steps of unconditional love. Remember that the breath contains energy. When you breath, you charge your body with energy. This charging of the body with energy is directly proportional to the speed and fullness of your breathing. The shallower and slower the breath, the less energy there is within you. The fuller and faster you breath, the more your body is charged with energy. By breathing fast and full, you charge your body with enough energy to bring all the suppressed emotions to the surface where they can be pleasurably and joyously integrated using the five steps of unconditional love.

You may think that doing the fast and full breath would draw attention in a public place but it usually doesn't. I have used this breath successfully in restaurants, on airplanes, and other places surrounded by people. I found that the people either didn't notice me or they choose to ignore it. Either way, I interpreted it as them supporting me being in joy. If you don't find yourself comfortable breathing fast and full around strangers, find a place where you can. There is rarely a place where one cannot be alone for a few minutes or find people that will support them. You will not find this a problem.

PRACTICING THE FAST AND FULL BREATH

As with running, you may want to increase your breath rate slowly until you have reached a rate that is both comfortable and effective. As was said earlier, the rate for fast and full breathing is sixty plus breaths per minute. Just like sprint running, this is a short term breath with a maximum duration of three minutes. For most people, the duration will be somewhere around sixty to ninety seconds.

The secret to increasing your breath rate is to practice at just above your comfort rate. This creates a stretch for you so that the next attempt at the same rate will be easier and more comfortable.

A common problem in doing the fast and full breath is the inability to relax the exhale. When one increases their breath rate they tend to want to hurry the breath along, and that includes the exhale. People tend to blow the exhale out. One way around this is to initially practice the fast and full breath while laying on your stomach and chest. In this way, the weight of your body will assist the lungs in quickly exhaling without the necessity of your control. This is also a great way to build up the muscle power of your lungs. Another pointer is to focus on the inhale only.

Do not be discouraged if you are not successful at first. It may take a few attempts. Once you have mastered this breath, you will find the slow and full breath quite easy to do.

As a review, focus on the inhale, lay on your stomach and chest to assist the uncontrolled exhale, breath through your mouth, and chose a rate just above your comfort rate.

FAST AND SHALLOW BREATHING

The faster one breathes, the faster they integrate energies. The fuller one breathes, the more they activate and bring suppressed energies to the surface. So, fast and full breathing tends to quickly activate and simultaneously integrate suppressed energies that are keeping us from experiencing joy.

On the flipside of the coin, people stop breathing or they breathe in a shallow fashion to suppress emotions and patterns of energy. When you find yourself breathing in a shallow manner, you are either suppressing or repressing patterns of energy or attempting to hold back patterns of energy that are about to surface.

If patterns of energies are already activated and quite intense (you will know this by the discomfort you are experiencing), do the fast and shallow breath. This will quickly integrate the energies and alleviate the pain or discomfort. All patterns of energy are quickly integrated by the fast and shallow breath simply because the fast breath integrate quickly and the shallow breath brings little energy into the body to cause further activation of energies.

Simple discomforts like headaches, upset stomach, muscle cramps, can be easily integrated with the fast and shallow breath. As with the fast and full breath, people find it difficult to relax the exhale. There is also a tendency to not fully exhale each breath, and so some experience what is called "ballooning". This is where your lungs start retaining a little bit of air from each inhale until it is obvious that the lungs are quite filled with air. If this occurs, stop the fast and shallow breathing momentarily, inhale fully and exhale in a relaxed manner, then begin the fast and full breathing again.

The recommended way to learn this breath is the old steam engine method. The same way an old steam locomotive would pull away from the train station in an old movie, slowly going chug, chug, picking up speed at a steady rate until it is chugging real fast. Begin breathing slow and shallow, focusing on the inhale and allowing the exhale to go uncontrolled. As soon as you have a rhythm and feel comfortable at that speed, slowly increase your breath rate while maintaining your focus on the inhale. It may take a few attempts. I have never witnessed anyone doing it the first try, so don't be discouraged if it takes awhile. This is the most difficult of the three breaths. It is also the most useful in integrating patterns of energy when you are experiencing discomfort or pain.

The main breath used in the five steps is the slow and full breath. Fast and full and fast and shallow are both short term breaths used for a specific purpose. Once complete, return to and maintain the slow and full breathing.

CHOOSING THE BEST BREATHING TECHNIQUE
You have just begun learning the three breaths used in the five steps of unconditional love. These breaths are tools for you to carry and use throughout your life. Use them to assist yourself in creating and maintaining continued joy in your life from now on.

Choosing what breath to use is quite simple. After awhile you will know intuitively what breath to choose. Someday, the choice will be totally automatic.

SLOW AND FULL

The mainstay breath is the slow and full. Learn this breath and do it all the time. This means twenty four hours a day every day. This breath is your main source of energy. Yes, I know some say that we get energy from food, but we also get energy from the air we breath. The more fully we breathe, the less food we require and the more we are full of energy and aliveness.

As a daily kickstart, I recommend that everyone do at least one hour of the slow and full breathing (with the other five Steps) every morning upon awaking. During this hour, you may choose to use the other breaths as necessary. This gives you a head start by integrating all the patterns of energy that were activated during your dream state, while charging your body with energy and love.

Use the slow and full breath throughout your day. The more you use it, the more it becomes automatic. Later in the book we will discuss how you can remind yourself to do the five steps throughout the day.

FAST AND FULL

There are times in our lives when breathing slow and full is not enough. This is when we may want to choose to breathe fast and full.

Since I have been practicing the five steps of unconditional love, I have stopped drinking coffee and caffeinated beverages. There have been many times when I have had to work through the night and remain awake. While others relied on coffee and tea, I was able to stay wide awake by just breathing fast and full whenever I felt sleepy. This also works when I drive cross country at night. So, when you wake up in the morning, do a few minutes of slow and full and then a minute or two of fast and full to fully awaken yourself and charge your body with energy and love. Whenever You feel drowsy, do the fast and full breath.

Another use for the fast and full breath is when you are feeling depressed. Usually, depression occurs when some suppressed emotions from the past have been activated either by a similar scenario, an anniversary, or a similar or same person. When this happens, we unconsciously attempt to resuppress it. If it is strong, we end up tapping most of our energy and feel tired and listless.

The best thing to do is to find a place where you can allow yourself to experience these emotions if they should appear. Sit or lay down and be comfortable. Focus on your breathing (slow and full) and relax. Make sure you are in all of the five steps. When you are ready, do the fast and full breathing for as long as necessary. You may want to do one minute of fast and full and five minutes of slow and full while you experience the emotions joyfully; then another minute of fast and full followed by five minutes of slow and full until you are full of joy and vivacious again. Because the fast breathing facilitates quick integration, you may not have to do anything but breathe fast and full. You may not have to experience the emotions, as they will be integrating as fast as they are activating.

FAST AND SHALLOW
This breath is best to quickly integrate any activated patterns of energy. For example, if the above procedure has activated a pattern of energy that was more intense than desired, you

could immediately do the fast and shallow breath and it would tone down the intensity by integrating the pattern of energy.

Whenever you experience pain of any kind, use the fast and shallow breath and it will integrate the patterns of energy that were the cause. Most unexplained pain is from the resistance to the flow of energy. The resistance comes from unconsciously suppressing emotions (repression). Wherever in the body that the emotion or energy was suppressed is where the pain will be felt.

If the emotion was grief, most likely it would have been suppressed in the organs related to the expression of grief. These are the sinuses, the eyes, the nose, the mouth and throat, and the lungs. Any pain in these areas would most likely be from suppressed grief. The common cold is just the manifestation of suppressed grief. I have personally nipped in the bud many so-called colds by just crying and doing the five steps.

Anger and rage are normal and natural emotions. In our society, they are shunned as inappropriate. So, most people suppress their rage and anger. Many are not even aware that they are suppressing rage or anger. This is called repression. These suppressed energies usually manifest as headaches, neck aches, back aches, stomach aches, nausea and even vomiting. Fear manifests itself in the legs. Tension in any muscle is from suppression of an emotion or action. We will talk more about these later on. For now it is only important to know that the fast and shallow breath will usually tone down or alleviate most pains and discomforts. If they don't integrate you may want to investigate further as to their cause.

To simplify choosing the correct breath for the situation, use the Breath Selection Chart. Be aware that the chart is only a guideline and at times you may be intuitively guided to use a different breath.

When using the different breaths to manage particular patterns of energy, you will find it beneficial to breath into those areas of the body. If an activation is above your waist, breath into your chest. If an activation is below your waist, breath into your abdominal area. Even though the air goes to the same place when you breath this way, the muscles used are different and it makes the breath more effective.

When you are in an intense experience, it may be difficult to remember this chart. You might want to photocopy it and carry a copy with you at all times until you are familiar with the full uses of the breaths. For most of your life, you will automatically be doing the very simple and uncomplicated slow and full breath. It is only those few times when something very intense may manifest that the other breaths will be a better choice. If you cannot decide which breath is best, stick with the slow and full.

As a quick review, the breath is circular and connected, beginning the inhale as soon as the exhale is complete and allowing the exhale to begin as soon as the inhale is complete.

Focus on the inhale and allow the exhale to be totally uncontrolled, relaxed and free.

If you find yourself not breathing, you are in fear, so BREATHE!

If you are having difficulty with any of these breaths, go back and review this chapter. Although breathing is not the most important of the five steps, it must be mastered.

BREATH SELECTION CHART

EXPERIENCE	*BREATH*
Discomfort	Fast and shallow
Drowsiness	Fast and full
Emotional intensity	Fast and shallow
Fear	Slow and full
Headaches	Fast and shallow
To Intensify Emotions	Fast and full
Muscle aches	Fast and shallow
Nervousness	Slow and full
Pain	Fast and shallow
Sleepiness	Fast and full
Tenseness	Slow and full
Toothache	Fast and shallow

CHAPTER SIX

Step Two
Complete Relaxation

Suppression of energies in your body causes tension. This tension lodges itself in the organs and muscles of suppression. Suppressed grief causes tension in the sinuses, throat, and lungs. Suppressed anger and rage causes tension in the back, neck, head, arms, and stomach, while fear usually tenses the back and leg muscles. These are the most common places that energy is suppressed.

It takes an enormous amount of energy to create and maintain tension in the human body. You could say that for every energy in motion that is suppressed, the body has to use an equal and opposite amount of energy to suppress it. This makes for an inefficient operation of the human body. It is similar to driving your car for years with the parking brake on. Once these patterns are freed up through integration, your body will have more energy available to you.

Complete relaxation is a target goal that will be achieved somewhere down your path to joy. It is when your body is completely free of tension or suppressed energies. Until that time, you will notice how more and more relaxed you are becoming. The more relaxed you are, the more energy is available to you. Some benefits of this is greater awareness, less need for sleep or rest, higher sports achievements, greater clarity, higher scholastic achievements and more pleasurable sexual experiences.

Practicing the second step of the five steps of unconditional love is simple. Be aware of tension in your body and relax it. Have more body awareness. All tension is fear related. We suppress energies because we fear punishment, rejection, hurt, loss of love and loss of approval.

When I used to teach flying, I discovered that it was difficult to teach in the airplane until I was able to get the student relaxed. Relaxing the student meant making him or her feel safe while flying. The most feared experience in an airplane is to have the engine stop. To instill a feeling of safety in the airplane, I would fly five miles from the airport and climb to about three thousand feet above the ground. Then I would pull the throttle back to idle speed and let the student fly the airplane all the way back to the airport. Once the student saw that the plane was still flyable with the engine stopped, he or she would relax and be able to absorb more information in a shorter period of time.

When students did their first approaches to landings, they always tensed up. As the airplane got closer to the ground, their shoulders would rise up and their hands would squeeze the control wheel tightly. They would lose the feel of the airplane and begin over-correcting. The tension was from fear. All I did was to tell them to drop their shoulders, relax and take a deep breath and exhale. It made all the difference.

Raising our shoulders is a standard reaction to fear. Observe yourself and others and you will see. An easy demonstration is to jump into a cold shower. Once in the cold water, observe your shoulders. Are they up? Almost everyone fears the cold. That is why your shoulders go up in the cold. We learned to fear cold from our parents and those around us. Simple statements like: You could catch a death of a cold, you could freeze to death, you could catch pneumonia and die tell the subconscious EGO defense system that cold is deadly. It is a life threatening situation. Anytime the EGO defense system senses this, it immediately goes into a fear reaction, whether from cold, flying in a small airplane or whatever.

Fear creates tension and tension creates loss of available energy, health and joy. When we are tensed, we tell the EGO that there is danger and the tension prevails. When we are relaxed we tell the EGO that we are safe and relaxation prevails. This system of feedback also works with the breath. When we are not breathing (or breathing very shallow), we are telling the EGO that we are in fear and the body tenses and shallow breathing continues. By breathing fully, freely and connectedly, we are telling the EGO that we are safe and the body leaves the defensive posture and relaxes into more joy.

Understanding the second step is vitally important. Doing it is more important. Actualizing complete relaxation is simply being aware of your body language and obvious tensions you are holding, and relieving the tension by relaxing your whole body. Surrender and allow the energies to move through your body and to move you.

Understand that you can be standing at full attention and your body can be fully relaxed. Tension is the resistance to the flow of energies in motion. Relaxing your body will allow these energies to flow and integrate moment by moment.

When you are fully relaxed, your muscles will be soft and pliable. Contrary to the beliefs of sports enthusiasts, hard muscles are not as strong as soft muscles. Hard muscles are in tension and so some of the energy available to those muscles is being used against the flow and purpose of those muscles. Soft and pliable muscles have no tension and so all the energy available to those muscles is used efficiently.

Just by breathing slowly and fully, your body will relax to some degree. Laying down and scanning the body muscle by muscle, and relaxing each muscle will bring you closer to complete relaxation. Popular places that we hold tension is in the neck, shoulders, upper and lower back, stomach, face, hands, legs, and groin. If you just scan and relax those areas, your level of complete relaxation will improve greatly.

By having a digital wrist watch with an hourly alarm, you can reminded yourself to check just how relaxed you are. Most painful tensions are usually the product of accumulated tensions. By checking yourself every hour and effecting relaxation every hour, you prevent pain and create joy. So, right now, lay down and scan your body. See just how much tension you are holding and relax that tension. Remember to breath slow and full. Practice this until you have mastered it enough to do it hourly while standing or sitting at your place of employment.

Complete relaxation is the absences of tension in your body. Tension is a reaction by your EGO defense system to a perceived life threatening or damaging experience. Most perceptions are in error due to early life programming. Just by telling your EGO defense system that you are safe will reduce tension and promote relaxation. What I say to my subconscious is the following: "RAJA, GO TO CONDITION GREEN, CANCEL RED ALERT, I AM SAFE." Your subconscious controls your EGO defense system. If you are feeling tense, fearful, uncomfortable in your body, nausea, light headed, dizzy or out of your body, you might be in fear. Tell your subconscious to "GO TO CONDITION GREEN, CANCEL RED ALERT". Most of the time, we are in some level of fear, so doing this command could only benefit you. I recommend you do it whenever you want or feel it is appropriate.

Certain yoga practices are very effective in releasing and integrating tensions in the body. Of these postures, the plow is my favorite. I do it at least once a day. I find it very pleasurable.

To do the plow, just lay flat on your back. Gently lift your legs over your head as if you were to touch your toes to the floor behind your head. Do not force yourself as this is a posture of relaxation. Just allow the weight of your legs to pull you over slowly.

The tension in your back and leg muscles (all your suppressed energy) will slowly release and flow through your hands, your feet and/or your head. As long as you breathe and experience the energies as patterns of energy and not pain, the experience will be almost ecstatic. Remain in this posture until all the energy flows have stopped.

For most people, doing the plow early in the morning may be difficult due to being immobile all night. I recommend you do the plow only after being mobile for a few hours. At first attempt, the plow may seem difficult or even impossible. Like everything else, it will become easier with practice. You may want to ask a yoga instructor for assistance and guidance.

A variance of the plow is what I call the inverted plow. I do it when there is no available room to do the plow. It is easy and you may want to do this first before attempting the plow.

Sit on the floor or flat surface with your legs straight out and together. Let your head, neck and upper torso lean forward using the weight of your upper body to do this. Again, like the plow, don't force movement, but allow gravity to do it all while you focus on breathing and relaxation.

Clasp your hands behind your head and allow the weight of your arms to move your head and torso down closer to the ground. Do not pull on your head or neck, but just allow the weight of your arms to do it all while you remain relaxed and breathing circular and connected.

You will notice your neck and back muscles and the rear leg muscles stretching slowly. As they do, the suppressed energy held in the muscles will slowly and pleasurably release and flow through the feet or head or both. Remain in this posture until all the energy flow has stopped.

When there is no way to sit or lay down, another variance is to do the inverted plow standing up. Just do as you would for the inverted plow, but stand with your legs together and your knees locked.

All in all, complete relaxation is simple and easy. The important thing is to be aware of your tension and practice relaxation at least once every hour. Body awareness is essential as is breathing fully and freely and connectedly.

CHAPTER SEVEN

Step Three
Awareness In Detail

Life is like a spectrum with total joy at one extreme and total fear at the other. The more we are in fear, the more we are out of touch with our feelings. Feelings are our emotions, our pains, and our pleasures. In order to become less in fear we must choose to become more aware. The more aware we become the less in fear we are. The more aware we are, the more joy we experience in our lives.

Joy is the awareness and experience of integrated energy flowing in our body. In order to facilitate the integration of our suppressed patterns of energy, we must first be aware of them. How can one redecorate a house if he or she won't look at the furnishings? In the same way, we cannot choose what we do and do not want in our life and body if we won't allow ourselves to experience the choices. Everything is a choice. Nothing is predestined. Everything can be changed, but before one can change something, they must first be aware of what it is.

When we are in fear, we tend to focus out of our bodies. Our focus becomes narrow and limited. When we are in fear. this is an automatic reaction. It is part of our survival mechanism. Breathing shallow, tensing up and limiting our awareness are all automatic reactions of our survival mechanism, the EGO defense mechanism. These reactions also feed the survival mechanism to prolong the fear reaction.

When the EGO defense mechanism senses we are breathing shallow, tensed up and in limited awareness, it believes we are doing it because we are in fear and sustains that fear reaction. Fear creates the fear reaction (shallow breathing, tension, loss of awareness) and the fear reaction feeds and sustains the fear perception. By breathing fully and freely, relaxing, and becoming fully aware in detail, the ego defense mechanism thinks we are not in fear and cancels all defensive measures. This puts us closer to the joy extreme of the spectrum, the extreme we want to live in full time.

Being around fearful people will trigger a fear reaction. Our subconscious telepathically senses others' fear. When enough people in close proximity are sensed to be in fear, our EGO defense mechanism will automatically go into a defense posture until it is convinced that we are safe. It can be difficult to maintain a safe posture when one is in a city where most people are in chronic fear. This is where the five Steps of unconditional love works well. Doing the five steps once an hour should keep you out of fear and in joy. If you are in the middle of a large metropolitan area, you may find it necessary to do the five steps as much as every fifteen minutes.

You may think the five steps is like meditation. Not so! Meditation is being in a blissful state by transcending the body or escaping the problems and stress of daily life. The five steps of unconditional love is being in joy while being fully in your body and experiencing life to the fullest. The only way to do this is by being fully aware of your body as it experiences life.

Before moving on, let us review "patterns of energy". In our bodies, we experience many sensations: taste, smell, touch, sight, hearing, emotions, pain, ecstasy, hot, cold, etc. Every sensation we experience is the result of a pattern of energy. Every thought is carried by a pattern of energy and is associated with a pattern of energy

Since thought is creative, when we name a pattern of energy, we maintain that experience through belief. A belief is a structure of thoughts about an experience. If one was to experience pain and say: "This is pain", the thought that it is pain will maintain the pain. By perceiving the pain only as a pattern of energy, the pattern of energy is able to flow and it will be easier for the pain to subside.

Many pains begin as a slight sensation. Our EGO defense system identifies it as a "pain" and begins unconsciously to resist it (Many of us also do this consciously). This resistance to the flow of energy causes an ever increasing pain. What could have been a slight discomfort for a short period, has now built up to an intensely painful experience. Most headaches are created this way.

When we have consciously or subconsciously judged a sensation as wrong or bad, we resist it and create intense pain. The resistance to the flow of energy causes pain. We create our own pain and pleasures. By being aware of our patterns of energy and not judging, defining or naming them we can create great joy in our lives.

Most of us have chosen not to be aware of certain patterns of energy because we have judged them wrong or bad. The fourth step, "Integration into Ecstasy", is used to release all judgments we may have on patterns of energy. Before we can use the fourth step, we must first be aware of the patterns of energy we judged.

The first step to awareness in detail is to become fully aware of your body. The best way to do this is to lay down in a comfortable and peaceful place, preferably your bed at a time when you are alone. Once you have laid down and relaxed, do the circular connected breathing and complete relaxation as described in the previous chapters. Now, get out of your thoughts and focus on your body.

Start at the most sensitive part of your body and just focus on that place until you are experiencing the patterns of energy in that area of your body in detail. When you think you are experiencing them fully, go for more detail. You will discover sensitivities that you did not think existed. Keep breathing and remain fully relaxed. This will aid in your increased awareness in detail.

Once you are experiencing awareness in detail at that point on your body, move to the next most sensitive point and again do as described in the last paragraph. Continue this until you are experiencing awareness in detail throughout your body.

You will discover feelings and sensations in places on your body that you never knew existed. Every place on and in your body is flowing with life and energy. When one is experiencing this aliveness and energy flow with awareness in detail, there is no need to do anything else but be and enjoy yourself as you are.

For many of us, we were taught early in life to ignore, deny and disassociate from our feelings and emotions. After we learned this, we practiced it for many years. Don't expect to just stop your numbness denial and disassociation of your energies immediately. It may take awhile to experience full awareness in detail. Practice makes perfect. So practice!

Once you have practiced being aware of the patterns of energy in your whole body for awhile, it will be easy to maintain full body awareness at all times, no matter where you are or what you are doing. Later, you will be shown how, in a few seconds every hour, you will be able to practice the five steps. Awareness in detail as well as the other steps will be second nature to you.

Most illness is caused by the suppression of energies in the body which in turn cause the breakdown and failure of cells and organs. As an example, the cause of the common cold has eluded the scientific community. This is because the common cold is not caused by a germ or organism. It is caused by the suppression and repression of grief or crying. When we cry, we use the eyes, sinuses, lungs, and throat. When we suppress crying, the E-motions or energies in motion are stopped at the organs of expression: the eyes, the sinuses, the lungs, and the throat. These organs, being overcharged with this high energy begin to break down on the cellular level.

Mucous forms, the sinuses and throat inflame, sneezing becomes a way for the body to use the suppressed energies quickly. If one is aware of the first symptoms of the so called common cold, it can be totally avoided. Whenever I become aware of a sneeze or some sadness or sniffles, I watch a sad "tear jerker" movie and cry through it. I identify a sneeze as my body's way of integrating sadness without crying and so I now enjoy sneezing. I see sneezing as a natural experience and not the sign of illness. Becoming aware of suppressed patterns of energy early on will stop any illness or disease before it has a chance to cause any problems.

Many religions and social beliefs view the human body as evil. For this reasons, people who are in the effect of these beliefs may find it very uncomfortable to be in their bodies. How they experience their bodies can be equated to someone driving their automobile by remote control. One practice I recommend to aid in being fully in your body is to put your hands on the top of your head and focus on your big toes. Once you are fully in awareness in detail of your big toes, move up your focus and you will experience awareness in the other parts of your body.

Patterns of energy you will experience in your body as you perfect awareness in detail will vary. Emotions are not the only patterns of energy that you will become aware of. Here is a short list of the most common patterns of energy:

COMMON PATTERNS OF ENERGY

feeling cold	feeling hot	visions
fear	itching	illness
twitching	blinking	pressure
nausea	sleepiness	pain
sneezing	sadness	grief
anger	rage	hunger
tastes	smells	sounds
sexual arousal	unique sensations	
dryness of the mouth		

Once you have mastered awareness in detail, you can experience more by doing less. People in suppression tend to gravitate to exciting experiences that create high adrenaline flow in their bodies. They like scary movies, amusement park rides, flying airplanes, fast cars and racing, sex, and drugs such as cocaine. These people have a feeling threshold that must be exceeded before they can feel anything. They need the excitement or drugs to feel alive. With the five steps, you need nothing. You are autonomously in joy anytime you are in the five steps of unconditional love

CHAPTER EIGHT

Step Four
Integration Into Ecstasy

Integration brings one into integrity with one's self and the world. When one is denying and disassociating with their own thoughts and patterns of energy, they are being dishonest with themselves and others. For every lie, one must build a *de"fence"* around it. This uses much of the conscious mind leaving little for enjoyment. When one is in defense, they are in fear of being discovered. The more in fear they are, the less in joy they can be.

The thoughts and patterns of energy that one denies and disassociates with are those they have judged as wrong or bad. It is the judgment and the fear of punishment for having these thoughts and energies that causes one to deny and disassociate with them. This denial and disassociation causes suppression and repression of energies.

Integration is the opposite of segregation. Segregation is basically judgment or comparing what is to something it is not and coming up with a result of "good", "bad", "right" or "wrong". Judgment causes separation, fear and hostility just as segregation has in the United States and the world. Segregation brings us fear and integration brings us joy.

When a pattern of energy is integrated, it is allowed to flow and the fear that held it disperses. This flow of energy creates a feeling of joy. If the integration is done continuously, the joyous experience will be ecstatic. This is why the fourth step is named: Integration into ecstasy. Just as ecstasy in love making is due to the enormous flow of energy through the body during climax, so the ecstasy one experiences during integration has the same source. When integration occurs, the suppressed energies are released to flow. This flow of energy can be experienced ecstatically.

There are two types of integration experiences. One where the pattern of energy disappears and the other where the pattern of energy remains but is now pleasurable.

The first type is the most common. You have a pain or discomfort and when it is integrated, it disappears totally. The second type refers to patterns of energy that are normal and natural to us but we have made them wrong or bad and so when they appear we feel discomfort. One you may have experienced already is a dryness of your mouth when you first practiced the first step of the five steps of unconditional love.

This dryness of the mouth is natural. Because our subconscious sees it as wrong, it becomes uncomfortable. Once we let go of the judgment of the experience the dryness remains and the discomfort goes. This works with every experience in life that we have judged as wrong or bad.

Some people associate smells, tastes, sounds and other sensations with traumatic experiences. When they sense them, they

91

react. Consciously integrating the patterns of energy will make them pleasurable experiences. The taste, smell or whatever will still be sensed, but it will be pleasurable now. Until one lets go of the judgment, they are giving their power to create joy in their lives to an object or experience they have little control over. Remember, you have the choice to be in joy all the time by practicing integration.

Integration into ecstasy is done by effecting the thought, spiritual, energy and physical bodies. By the use of certain thought patterns called "integration techniques" we can initiate integration. By commanding the assistance of a "Holy Trinity" (see page 96), integration is effected effortlessly by ascended masters through our spiritual body. Our energy body responds by allowing the suppressed energies to flow. We feel this flow in our physical body as ecstasy.

INTEGRATION TECHNIQUES
There are at least fifty known integration techniques. Out of these I have chosen the ones that are the most effective. If you discover other integration techniques and they work for you, use them. The integration techniques are basically short phrases and thoughts that have the power to break us free from fear, judgment and duality. Choose the ones from this list that work best for you and memorize them. Sometimes just saying the phrase is enough to pop us into ecstasy. Other times, we must do what the phrase says, such as "love it unconditionally", or "compare it only to itself". Here are the integration techniques:

I AM THIS PATTERN OF ENERGY This is the most effective of all the techniques I have ever used. It is simple and requires nothing more than making the statement "I am this pattern of energy". When we make something wrong, deny or disassociate with it, we are attempting to say that IT is not

92

ours or IT is not a part of us. That causes separation and pain. By saying, "I am this pattern of energy" we are making IT okay to be a part of us and so it flows and integrates almost instantly.

Since thought is creative, I recommend you don't say what the pattern of energy is perceived as. For example, if you are feeling pain, don't say you are in pain as that will hold the pain in state. Energies that are suppressed, controlled or repressed will cause pain and damage to body tissue. Saying, "I am this pattern of energy" you release the judgment on that pattern of energy and it flows or integrates.

IT COULD BE INFINITELY MORE INTENSE, SO BE THANKFUL THAT IT IS ONLY AS INTENSE AS IT IS. This one is self explanatory and has worked very well for me and others. Say you have a slight headache. Remember when you had a raging migraine. Be thankful that it is only a slight headache and not a migraine. Use this with all experiences. If you lose five dollars, be thankful it wasn't five hundred dollars or five hundred thousand dollars.

GO DIRECTLY FOR ENJOYING IT You have the choice of either suffering through or enjoying every moment of your life, so you might as well choose to enjoy it. Just by choosing to enjoy an experience can bring the experience to one of joy. How one responds to every situation in life is a choice. We have been taught not to enjoy certain experiences and so we choose to suffer even when we don't have to. Don't do what people expect you to do. Do what you want to do. Be spontaneous! Choose joy!

CHANGE THE CONTEXT THAT YOU ARE HOLDING IT IN If you are being tickled on the arm with a feather, it is fun and pleasurable. If a fly is tickling your arm, it is displeasing and irritating. Why? It is the same sensation only it is in a different context. Don't make the fly wrong or bad. It is just a fly and when you change the context, the fly on your arm will feel as pleasurable as a feather.

CANCEL CONDITION RED! GO TO CONDITION GREEN! This is one we all can use. Our subconscious EGO defense system is constantly identifying (in error) life/death issues. When it does, we go into fight or flight reaction. We can feel the fear and the rage energy bubbling up in our gut. Just talk to your subconscious and tell it that you are safe. What I do is say: "Raja, go to condition green! Cancel red alert! Integrate all activated rage energy now!"

IT IS NOT A LIFE OR DEATH ISSUE Many of us see most of life's challenges as life or death issues. Something as simple as losing a few dollars can really put a damper on some people's joy. This comes from the belief that we need money to live...and so, it also means if we don't have money we will die. Untrue! This life/death perception goes with many other common experiences in life and just by becoming aware of this and stating that it is not a life/death issue will integrate the energies.

COMPARE IT ONLY TO ITSELF The discomfort you are experiencing is due to judgment, the comparing of something to something it isn't. See its perfection and uniqueness. Compare it only to itself and the result can only be that it is perfect. This is a good one for anger. We are taught, by our parents and society, to get angry at anyone or anything that is wrong or bad. Let go of the judgment and the anger is gone also.

ALLOW IT TO BE THERE Love it without judgment. It is in your life experience, so love it unconditionally. Allow it to be there and enjoy it. Don't resist it as that is how things get stuck in the first place. When you try to get rid of something it won't integrate. You must embrace it fully or it will stay until you do. <u>The more you want to get rid of something the more it stays stuck. Just allow it to be there and it will integrate</u>.

LIGHTEN UP AND ENJOY IT Most people believe that acting serious is important in getting certain jobs done. Not so! Being happy and joyous usually makes one more effective in accomplishing their purpose. I have yet to see where being serious ever helped any situation. This includes having to make an emergency landing with an airplane full of people which I did in Arizona in 1990.

There is a story of a monk that was chased to a cliff by a tiger. He climbed down a vine to escape the jaws of the predator. As the vine began unrolling itself and in the face of death, he reached over to a strawberry bush and enjoyed the last few moments of his life eating the delicious strawberries. He could have experienced those moments in pain and fear. He chose not to. He chose to be in joy and you can also.

DON'T MAKE YOURSELF WRONG Making errors or mistakes is a natural and normal part of the learning experience. If you were never allowed to stumble or fall when you were a child you probably would not be walking now. See mistakes and errors as stepping stones of learning and move on.

GIVE UP THE NEED TO BE GOOD AND RIGHT Many of us, as children, were punished (sometimes severely) when we were wrong or bad. From this experience, a child learns that in order to live, it must always be good and right. Being good and right becomes a life/death issue. In some, this causes a compulsive need to be good and right. This need is driven by a powerful survival energy, rage. Whenever this type person sees him/herself as being wrong or bad, it activates suppressed rage from childhood.

It is important to identify this compulsive reaction as soon as possible. Then, tell your subconscious EGO defense system and yourself that you are safe. Tell yourself that being wrong and bad is safe and pleasurable. Repeat this statement over and over until you have yourself convinced and the patterns of energy are integrated.

USING A HOLY TRINITY
A holy trinity is three ascended masters working in concert to assist you. A Holy Trinity has the power of synergy. Their abilities are unlimited. I have watched people in pain move into ecstasy in less than a minute by asking their Holy Trinity to assist them.

I have worked extensively with Jesus, Babaji (from "Autobiography of a Yogi") and Kwan Yin and recommend you use them as your Holy Trinity. You may also chose any close spiritual friends since we are all ascended masters. To use your Holy Trinity, you would command: Holy Trinity, assist me in integrating this(or these) pattern(s) of energy now." After stating that, say: "I am this pattern of energy." or "I am these patterns of energy".

If you haven't chosen your Holy Trinity earlier in the book, then now is the best time to choose your Holy Trinity. Fill in the blanks. You may change your selections of ascended masters or even have more than one Holy Trinity.

MY HOLY TRINITY

Saint No. 1:_____

Saint No. 2:_____

Saint No. 3:_____

Anytime you are not in joy, it is because you have separated yourself from yourself and others and you are in fear. Choose one or more of the integration techniques and use them immediately while doing the other Five Steps of Unconditional Love. The more you do this the easier it gets. The more you do this, the more joy and light you bring into your life.

Apply these integration techniques to every area of your life and not just your bodily experiences. For example, you may be upset about being five hundred dollars in debt. Using "It could be infinitely more intense, so be thankful that it is only as intense as it is" as an integrative technique, basically you would be saying that it could be five thousand dollars and not five hundred. A forest fire burns out five houses. It could have been the whole neighborhood or a city.

You go to use the toaster and it doesn't work. Your initial reaction is to get angry at it. You compared it to a toaster that works and made it wrong. Your early programming was to get angry at anything or anybody that is wrong. Your body produces anger inappropriately. The anger is useless in getting the toaster to work and it pulls you out of your center. You could proceed on with the anger or you could use "compare it only to itself". When you compare it only to itself it has to be perfect. There is no anger created and any anger that has surfaced gets integrated. You are now clear of any emotional roller coaster and can address the problem effectively. Oh, the plug is out of the wall socket. Much easier and more joyous.

I once made a small card for a friend with the following message on it: "You are expressing anger towards me so you must have compared me to someone that I am not and made me wrong. Please compare me only to myself and you will see that I am the perfect daughter that you love and cherish unconditionally."

I instructed my friend to give it to her daughter so that the daughter would either show or read the card to her whenever she got angry. It worked.

Integration into ecstasy is getting rid of judgment and the resultant separation and pain it causes. Apply these integration techniques in all realms of your life, not just your body. We are all just reflections of each other. How you see life and others is how you view yourself, consciously and unconsciously.

Without fear and judgment, love flows unconditionally within ourselves, and between ourselves and others. By practicing integration, you will be teaching it by example.

CHAPTER NINE

Step Five
Do It Now, Be Spontaneous

All through our lives we are taught to think before we act. Will our actions please those we are associated with? Will this be pleasing to others? All through our lives we are taught to think about others and how they will react to what we do. The spontaneity we had as little children was lost through our fear of disapproval and punishment.

To be spontaneous is to be yourself. To act as others want you to is to be in an act, not being yourself, but being a lie to please others. Do as others want you to do and you are just another robot. Those around you control you by your fear of disapproval and punishment. You have given up your true self to be a rubber stamp for the want of a little approval or conditional love from others.

You are a unique being. You are the only one like you in the whole universe. By being yourself, by being spontaneous, you maintain your individuality and uniqueness. Break free from the belief that your love comes from outside of yourself.

Break free from your need of approval from others. Break free from your co-dependence of others. Love yourself unconditionally and do as you please, for yourself, and if it happens to please others, okay...if not, that's okay also.

Others love you the way you love yourself. When you are unconditionally loving and approving of yourself, others will be also. This is not theory, but a proven reality. When you are not unconditionally loving and approving of yourself, you will find the people you attract will be judgmental and disapproving. How one loves themself is how others will love them. Everyone is a reflection of yourself.

Your thoughts and actions create. When you judge, disapprove and punish yourself you are demonstrating to the universe that this is the way you want to be treated. Since the universe gives us whatever we want, it sends us those people that are judgmental, disapproving and punishing. Even people that don't normally have those attributes will manifest them if you telepathically command them. Your subconscious beliefs are telepathic commands for everyone in your reality. Change your beliefs and your telepathic commands and reality will change. Use the Command Subconscious Programs in chapter two to accomplish this.

Those of us who are unconditionally loving and approving of ourselves are demonstrating to the universe that we want to be treated that way. We attract unconditionally loving and approving people to us. How people treat us is a barometer or gauge that shows us how we treat ourselves. You will know you are unconditionally loving to yourself when those around you love and accept you unconditionally.

To assist you in becoming spontaneous, ask all those you associate with to allow you to be spontaneous. You may find that many will feel uncomfortable or be afraid to do this, and you will have to choose between yourself and your freedom or them. In the beginning you may have to start small, spending the majority of your time with those who support you in being spontaneous. Key people that must be allowing are those you are intimate with. These include your lover, spouse, intimate friends and family. Many have trouble with family and have to separate from them until the family members find loving and accepting you unconditionally more important than controlling you.

There are many ways to be spontaneous: in action, in emotions, in speech, in thought, in decisions. The key power word here is ALLOW. In order for you to be spontaneous, you must ALLOW yourself the freedom to be spontaneous. You must allow yourself to say, think, emote and do whatever you desire in the moment without thinking about it first.

I have known many adults who wanted to skip down the street with me but felt self conscious. They chose not to because of their fear of disapproval. Something as simple as swinging on the swing in a playground brought great fear that disabled them from having fun.

Have you ever wanted to sing or dance but were afraid that people would laugh at you? So you didn't do what you wanted to and were controlled by those ignorant and abusive people that you probably will never see again. This is your life to do as you please. Just because others have given up their power doesn't mean you have to. Be yourself!

I have lived in a motor home for years and have parked in places where water is scarce. It was at times and in places such as these that I learned to clean my plates and eating utensils by licking them. What I discovered is that licking my plate was fun and delicious. Besides being able to clean everything with very little water, I was able to do something I enjoy. Something I was told not to do as a child.

Since I love and approve of myself unconditionally, I can lick my plate whenever I feel like it. I enjoy licking the plates after eating pancakes, Chinese food, Italian food, ice cream, cake and pie. I lick my plate at home, at other peoples' homes and in first class restaurants. I don't always lick my plates, but I do it when I want to.

Many believe that if they act appropriately in specific situations they will always be secure, loved or approved of. In the business world many believe this is the way to be. The most successful business people are the ones that are creative and spontaneous. Creativity and spontaneity seem to go hand in hand. Squelch spontaneity and the creative flow is shutdown. Businesses that allow their employees to be more themselves usually become the beneficiary of their employees' creativity and spontaneity. Communication, a necessary component in any business, is impeded by the control of spontaneity.

Being spontaneous is being honest and in the moment. If you are in an act then you are not being you. If you are upset at someone but afraid to express your emotions then you are in a lie. Even if you say you are angry without expressing the emotions it is a lie. It is important to express your emotions when you feel them and in the moment that they arise. To hold them until a more appropriate time is damaging to yourself, and not being spontaneous.

Suppressing grief does the same thing as does suppression of rage or laughter. Just know that whatever you are feeling in the moment is okay and to express it in that moment. Our emotions are natural and normal and serve us. Just because you or others may not think them logical or appropriate is no reason for suppression. Emotions are not a product of logic, so don't expect them to appear at logical times and events.

Our emotions will arise at different times, with different intensities and for different lengths of time. The reason they appear is of no consequence. All that matters is that we express them fully and spontaneously.

There is a source of some of our grief. We are Masters and Gods and kings and queens, yet we live like paupers and serfs. It is a great loss we know and until we regain our powers and abilities, we will grieve for it. I grieve almost everyday. Not only for myself, but for all my brothers and sisters and the planet. I know someday the grieving will end, but until that day, I will cry.

Because there is such a defined structure of rules for when and where we can express emotions, we, as a people, have created events where we can vent our suppressed emotions. At most sporting events it is accepted to shout and scream and be rowdy. In the theater and at movies it is acceptable to laugh and cry. A little child is spontaneous and expresses emotions when and wherever it wants. It needs no sporting event or movie to relieve its emotions. Be like a little child and free your emotions. Be honest and in the moment. The point of power is in the present moment. The only way to enter the kingdom of heaven is as a little child.

When we make or adopt rules that limit us and prevent us from being spontaneous, we have created a prison for ourselves. Those rules are manacles and chains that keep us from being free. It can be difficult to set yourself free from how you have been living for many years. Don't expect a total change instantly. Release yourself a little each day. Each day be a little more spontaneous. Each day do something else you want to do that you wouldn't allow yourself to do before now.

In intimate relationships, make rules to allow spontaneity to happen. There are usually large amounts of suppressed emotions that each partner is holding from childhood. An intimate relationship tends to activate those emotions on a daily basis. Because the emotions don't seem logical nor appropriate, they are re-repressed. Have an understanding that all emotions expressed are not a personal assault but a healthy way to spontaneously integrate old suppressed emotions. When your partner is expressing emotions, be the witness and not the receiver. See yourself as watching a movie or drama on TV. You will be touched by the honesty but not activated into retaliation. You can remain centered to support your partner in being spontaneous. Have your partner agree to allow you the same space. There will be times when both partners will be activated. Again, just be spontaneous and don't take personally what the other says or does. Be yourself and be a witness not only to your partner but to yourself.

Allow and promote your children to be more spontaneous. You will find that many of the rules we impose on our children we received from our parents. Most of them have little benefit and are usually based on fear and conditional love and approval. Weed out those rules and allow your children to be conscious and responsible human beings. Allow your children the freedom to hug and kiss whom they choose. Also allow them the freedom to refuse to hug or kiss whom they choose. Children are very intuitive and sensitive and they are human beings with rights also. Respect those rights.

LEARN TO SAY NO

A great block to spontaneity is the need to please others and get their conditional love and approval. As children, most of us were taught not to say no to our parents or adults. We were taught to be little obedient robots. If you find yourself saying yes when you mean no, it is time for you to say no even when you mean yes.

This is an exercise that breaks the habit and compulsion of saying yes when you mean no. It is simple! For one week, say no to every request from others. Even if you mean yes, say no. Reserve the choice of doing what is requested, but say no anyway. It is not the doing or not doing that creates fear of rejection or punishment, but the saying no. Make it a game and have fun with it.

Before beginning this exercise, explain to all those you relate to that you will be saying no to all their requests. Do this with all the people at your place of employment, your spouse, parents, friends and children. Show them this book and explain what you are doing. Tell them that you will be saying no to all of their requests even if you choose to do what they ask. Make it a game. Keep it light and fun. Create signals so that they know when you mean yes and when you mean no. If you truly mean no, you will just say no. If you mean yes, say no and pull on your ear lobe or take off your glasses or run your fingers through your hair. One of these simple gestures will be the signal that you mean yes. Since most people have a difficulty in saying no, you may want to enlist everyone in saying no also.

Once you have said no to everyone and everything for a week, you will find it easy to say no when you want to and mean it. The feedback you receive from others when you say no is an important factor in moving through this block. As you experience acceptance and love when you say no, it will reprogram your beliefs about saying no. When you can say no and have fun doing it, you will realize that you can say no to anyone, anytime and it will be okay.

Do this exercise now and anytime you find yourself not being able to say no when you want to. While you're saying no to everyone else, practice saying yes to yourself. Affirm your personal worthiness and spontaneity.

Procrastination is the opposite of doing it now. You may find yourself creating excuses to put off doing it now. They may even sound pretty convincing, but they are not. There is no reason, short of your own death, to not do it now.

We have been doing the steps of conditional love for almost all of our lives. Even though the five steps of unconditional love are simple, you may find difficulty in practicing and re-membering them. For this reason, I have set up an easy schedule to follow.

I first tried this with a friend. I hung an oven timer around my neck and every fifteen minutes, when it beeped, we both did the following procedure. And within an hour or two we were in a very high and joyous state of being. We were driving those around us up a wall with the beeping of the timer, but we were having a great time.

For under ten dollars you can buy a wrist watch that chimes every hour on the hour. Once you have memorized the five steps, doing them will take just seconds. Having the watch as a reminder, you can practice the five steps every hour. (There are also watches available with automaticically resetting countdown timers for $20.00 and up. Using one of them, you can do this practice every fifteen minutes.) When the watch chimes, stop what you are doing and do the following:

CIRCULAR CONNECTED BREATHING
Become aware of your breathing. Adjust it so it is full, free and circular and connected.

COMPLETE RELAXATION
Check your body for tension. Drop your shoulders if they are up. By taking a few deep breaths and focusing on relaxing, you can combine the first two steps.

AWARENESS IN DETAIL
Are you feeling any energy moving in your body? Do you feel alive? If not, focus on your body and become aware of the energies. This won't take long.

INTEGRATION INTO ECSTASY
Now that you are focused on your energies, are you experiencing any discomfort? If so, integrate these patterns of energy by using your favorite integration techniques. My favorites are: "I AM THIS PATTERN OF ENERGY" and asking my Holy Trinity to assist me in integrating these patterns of energy. Remember that patterns of energy won't integrate if you are trying to get rid of them. You must love them unconditionally and embrace them as yourself. Eventually, you will become aware of your patterns of energy and integrate them simultaneously.

DO IT NOW, BE SPONTANEOUS
Are you holding back with something? Is there something you want to say, do or express? Do it! Be it! Express it! Is there something you are doing that you really don't want to do but you are doing it to please someone else? Stop doing it now!

PRACTICE MAKES PERFECT

Once you practice these five steps for a day you will see and feel a wonderful improvement in your life: more joy, more aliveness, more effortlessness and fun. After a few days, it will take only seconds to check and maintain yourself in the five steps. Your energy will be high and joyous. Continue to do the five steps every hour, every day and you will experience total joy and prosperity in your life. Do this for twenty one days and the five steps should become automatic.

Be spontaneous! Be yourself! Don't put on an act to please anyone. You may find that wearing cosmetics is another way to please others. Who you are is not your looks or what you do, it's what you BE. BE yourself! BE spontaneous! BE in truth! BE in unconditional love of yourself! BE the special and unique being you came to this planet to be! BE your true and unique self now!

CHAPTER TEN

Morning Kickstart

Every night, as we sleep and dream, we activate patterns of energy. When we awake, these patterns of energy are right on the surface of our conscious awareness. If we don't integrate them when we awake, we will have to integrate them during the day by creating scenarios to do so. This can cause serious problems. By integrating them while we're still in bed, we start the day in joy and don't have to carry these patterns of energy with us. This really lightens one's load. Practicing the Five Steps before arising gives us a great head start.

This kickstart process may take a few minutes or an hour or more. Allow yourself enough time so that you are not rushed. When you awake, take care of your physiological needs (go to the bathroom). After you return to your bed, get comfortable and begin to breathe slow and full. Relax and become aware in detail. As the patterns of energy appear, integrate them using the integration techniques in chapter five.

Be spontaneous in your actions. If you feel like moving around, do so. Some people will feel more comfortable on their stomach and some like it better on their back. There are times when you may want to curl up into a fetal ball or hug your pillow. Cry if you feel it. Remember to stay in your body and in awareness in detail.

When you have integrated all the activated patterns of energy, you will be in joy. Your experience will be one of ecstasy or profound peace. As you breathe you should feel a glow of energy with every breath. You will feel like wanting to stay in bed and continuing the kick start forever. At this time you are complete and can get up and be active at anytime you choose.

Just because you are getting out of bed and being active doesn't mean you have to stop practicing the five Steps. You have just completed your kickstart. Maintain the joy by continuing to practice the five steps throughout your day. Put on your alarm wrist watch and check yourself every hour or every fifteen minutes.

CHAPTER ELEVEN

Integrating Pain

You have already read, earlier in this book, that pain is caused by the resistance to the flow of energy. This is true most of the time. Pain is also a way our body warns us of an injury or malfunction. Each type of pain takes a different procedure to facilitate relief. We will call the first type "energy pain" and the second type "alarm pain".

INTEGRATING ENERGY PAIN
There are times in our lives when large blocks of suppressed energy are activated at once. Activation of this type usually occurs during an anniversary of a traumatic experience, or the witnessing of a similar scenario or person involved in a past traumatic experience. This activation can cause pain and illness if the energies that have been activated are not brought to your awareness and integrated using the five steps.

Even though one may feel pain and discomfort or perceive being ill, they are actually going through a healing. Anytime suppressed energies have been activated and integrated, a healing is taking place. You have the choice of letting the patterns of energy integrate painfully or taking command of your experience and integrate them pleasurably though the use of the five steps.

Even when we are doing our five steps checklist every hour, there can be times when blocks of energies can be activated suddenly. When this happens, you will know it by your level of discomfort or pain. Respond to this immediately. The longer you delay your response, the more difficult it will be to integrate the patterns of energy and alleviate the pain or discomfort.

STEP ONE: Do not perceive the pain as something being wrong with you. Remember that thought is creative and if you think there is something wrong with you, there will be. Also, as soon as you perceive that something is wrong with you, your EGO defense system will go into survival mode and you will lose conscious control of your body.

STEP TWO: Perceive the experience as patterns of energy. Tell yourself and those around you that you are going through a healing.

STEP THREE: Breathe! Yes, by this time you probably will have discovered that you have forgotten to breathe. Don't make yourself wrong for this, just breathe....slow and full at first, then ease yourself into fast and shallow breathing.

STEP FOUR: Relax! You are safe. Just relax any tension in your body. Tell your subconscious to go to condition green and cancel red alert.

STEP FIVE: It goes without saying that you are aware of the patterns of energy. Now see them as patterns of energy and not pain. Experience them in detail. Where are they from? What color are they? What shape are they? Are they flowing or stagnant? If they are flowing, what type of motion do you perceive? Is it linear or circular, rhythmic, pulsating or steady? Is it thick or thin, heavy or light, slow or fast?

STEP SIX: Use your integration techniques. The best ones for this are to say: "I AM THESE PATTERNS OF ENERGY." and ASK YOUR HOLY TRINITY AND YOUR SUBCONSCIOUS TO INTEGRATE THESE PATTERNS OF ENERGY INSTANTANEOUSLY.

STEP SEVEN: Visualize these patterns of energy as flowing and integrating. Wanting these patterns of energy to be gone will block them from integrating, so just observe their movement, don't force it.

STEP EIGHT: Be spontaneous! Do whatever you have to do to facilitate the other steps. Do what you want to and not what others tell you to do. If those around you are not assisting you in your integration into ecstasy, either tell them to leave or you go somewhere else by yourself.

STEP NINE: Sometimes pain is due to spiritual possession by an evil being. To clear this, say: "God, depossess me now!" It is difficult to tell if you are possessed and it is so easy to request depossession, so make it standard policy to do at time of pain.

For the majority of your pain and illness experiences, if you catch them early the pain sensations will be quite low in intensity. And you will catch them early if you practice the Five Steps of Unconditional love on a regular basis. Sometimes, all it takes to relieve a pain or headache is to say: "I am this pattern of energy." Relax and breathe fast and shallow. The pain will subside almost immediately. Again, if you ignore the pain until it is intense, it will take longer for integration to occur. Also, if the patterns of energy are not integrated when they appear, there is a possibility that they will cause tissue inflammation and "Alarm Pain".

RELIEVING ALARM PAIN

You may have noticed that I didn't say "Integrating alarm pain" That is because its origin is different. It is not caused by resistance to the flow of energy, but is a warning signal to alert you of cellular damage in the body.

Because it is an alarm signal, it can be toned down in intensity or even shut off. Tell your subconscious that you are aware of the damage to your body or malfunction of your body and to shut off the alarm system. In the event of an injury, the Ego defense system will perceive you as under attack. For this reason, tell your subconscious to go to condition green. Cancel red alert! Tell it that you are safe.

Doing this will relieve the pain, or if nothing else, tone the pain down to a tolerable level. Another way to deal with physical pain is to change the context in which you are holding it. When I used to get dental work done, I never used Novocain. Instead, I saw the sensations as pleasurable and not painful.

Another way of looking at this technology is through a simple experiment. Take a bucket of ice cold water. Blindfold a friend and tell them you are going to put their hand in a bucket of hot water. When their hand touches the cold water they will experience it as boiling hot water because you have made the suggestion that it is hot and not cold.

In the same way, if you tell yourself that the sensations are pleasurable and not painful, eventually they can be pleasurable. Remember to relax. If you are tensed up, you are still telling yourself that the sensations are painful and so they will be. I have actually been able to enjoy a dentist jabbing those little fish hooks into the nerve of my tooth. It took much focus on my part and I remembered to breathe and relax.

If, after doing the above, you still feel pain, synthesize pain relievers into your body as described under SYNTHESIZING DRUGS. If you require a prescription drug, ask your local druggist to lend you one pill for a minute. Put it in the palm of your left hand and command your subconscious to scan the drug (by name) and synthesize it into every cell of your body as necessary to halt the pain. For over the counter pain killers, just go to the shelf and hold a closed package of the drug in your left hand and do the same.

These techniques work for ninety five percent of all pain and discomfort. I have found times when it wasn't enough. At those times, I had to revert to the use of an aspirin or two. If these techniques are not working for a particular pain or the pain hasn't subsided in a few days, you might want to consider seeing a professional for assistance as there are times when pain is a warning of a serious problem.

Now that you know this information is here, remember where it is, so that if pain appears, you will be able to access this information quickly.

CHAPTER TWELVE

Integrating Illness

Most illnesses are caused by the suppression of energies in the body. When these energies are concentrated in one organ or area it causes the cells in that organ or area to break down, fester, malfunction or die. Look at your skin when it is exposed to an overdose of solar energy (the Sun). It gets red. It hurts. It becomes inflexible. It blisters and delaminates. The skin is the largest organ in the body. The other organs in the body react the same way to high levels of energy.

Of the illnesses that are caused by the suppression of energies, sinusitis and the cold are the most common. These are caused by the suppression and repression of grief or crying energy. When one suppresses energy, it gets suppressed in the organs and muscles of expression. In this case, the sinuses, the eyes, the throat, and the lungs.

When I discovered this, I was able to shorten the term of a cold from a week to a day or two. My chronic sinusitis disappeared forever. Whenever I experience sneezing, usually the first signs of a cold, I focus awareness in detail on my sinuses for patterns of energy. I do the five steps of unconditional love until the patterns of energy are integrated. I also look at the calendar to see if it is an anniversary of a loss. If it is, I think of the loss and focus on it until I get in touch with the grief. Then I spontaneously express it and experience it.

I cry! I cry and I enjoy crying. You can also. I allow myself to sneeze and enjoy it. I don't make sneezing wrong or see it as a sign of illness. I see it as a sign that I am integrating grief in a healthy and pleasurable manner. I watch a movie that is a tearjerker for me. Movies effect people differently, so get a movie that gets you to cry. Watch the movie by yourself. Even if a friend is supporting you in crying, there may be some inhibition to crying with someone else around, so do it alone.

Many years ago I was told that a sore throat was caused by not saying something you wanted to say. It is true. When one holds back verbal expression, it suppresses that energy in the throat area and causes the tissue in that area to inflame, just like the skin does when it is exposed to an excess of solar energy.

Become aware of what it is you haven't been saying and express it.... not just intellectually, but with emotions also. If you are holding back, you probably are not practicing the fifth step, "Be Spontaneous". Who or what are you afraid of? Who are you looking to please? Give it up! Please yourself! Approve of yourself!

Stomach problems are usually caused by the overstorage of emotions. Sadness, anger and/or rage can cause an upset stomach or worse. Anything from a slight upset to vomiting to an ulcer can be caused by the suppression of emotions.

Look at what is going on in your life. Are you in a stress situation? Are you in chronic fear? Have you been allowing yourself to cry or get angry? Get in touch with what you are or are not doing that is causing your stomach problems and change them. Practice the Five Steps of Unconditional Love to integrate the patterns of energy in your abdominal area. Take steps to change your life so it is less stressful. Be spontaneous with your expressions of emotions and thoughts.

Some people hold their emotions in their large intestines. When they have some activated emotions to be expressed and integrated, emotions that they are resisting and holding back, they usually experience constipation. Constipation is the physical reflection of holding back your emotional stuff.

Again, the best, fastest and most pleasurable way to integrate constipation is to express your emotions. Be in the five steps. You should have them memorized by now. Do it now! The longer you wait, the more difficult it is for you to get in touch with your emotions.

To augment the end of your constipation, ask your subconscious to irrigate your colon and soften your stools so that you will be able to effortlessly eliminate them four hours from now. Make sure you are near a bathroom in four hours. You can make it five or six hours, what ever is convenient for you. Remember that you are in command of your body and your subconscious is responsible for the operation of the inner organs. Whatever you ask, your subconscious will accomplish.

INTEGRATING SUPPRESSED RAGE
Rage is an energy of survival. The lower energy center of the body is the survival center. It is located around the anus and the sex organs. By breathing into this area, one can activate

118

the rage energies into movement. They then travel up the back to the shoulders where they would build in intensity.

When the intensity of the energies around the shoulders builds to an uncomfortable level, halt the breathing into the groin area to stop any further increase of intensity. Breathing slowly and fully into the upper chest a few times will totally integrate the energies that were activated. This is called the "Rage Breath".

Rage is an energy that few talk about and even fewer want to experience. Most people avoid it like the plague. Rage is a killing energy. When substantial amounts of it are suppressed in the body, the body will manifest killing diseases, diseases that destroy the body. When enough of it is stored up, it usually appears as an uncontrollable outburst of rage, violence and destruction. Because rage is a natural and normal energy, most people have this potential.

RAGE BREATH
To do the "Rage Breath," lay stomach down on a bed. Rest your head on a pillow so that your air passages and your mouth are not blocked or restricted in any way. You will find that wrapping your arms around the pillow will free your lungs for full operation.

Your lungs operate by the movement of the diaphragm muscles. The air always goes into the lungs. By focusing on your groin area and moving the muscles in that area you will effect the diaphragm and activate rage simultaneously.

Using the fast and full breath (remembering to focus on the inhale and let the weight of your body assist in the exhale), do one hundred breaths or as many as you can. Stop when you either have done one hundred breaths, have activated a substantial amount of rage and are experiencing it in the shoulder area, or are exhausted.

Pause for a second and relax. Now, take a few slow and full breaths into the upper lungs and allow the patterns of energy in the shoulders to integrate. Repeat this process as many times as necessary to rid your body of all rage energies.

Now that you know this information is here, remember where it is so that if illness appears, you will be able to remedy it quickly.

CHAPTER THIRTEEN

Just a Few Commands For Love, Liberation And Ascension

When we were children we sourced our parents for our love. As teenagers we were trained to source a lover and finally to marry the source of our love. All this seeking and we still seem incomplete and unloved for the majority of our lives. Maybe it's time to stop seeking and go within.

When we were children and we were ill, we looked to our parents and doctors to nurse us back to health. As we matured spiritually, we sourced healers. Again we looked outside of ourselves for the source of our healing. There is a place within us that it the source of our love and a source of our healing. It is time for us to take back our powers of love and healing and become autonomous and fully empowered, to become one with God.

Jesus healed himself and then through his own self experiences learned to heal others. Many that were healed were possessed by evil beings. Jesus knew this because he could detect them in his body. The most powerful demons, anti-Christs and evil beings attempted to bring Jesus down. In their attempts, these beings only achieved to train Him in being a healer and a liberator.

Jesus learned that the source of most illness and disabilities was these evil beings, anti-Christs and demons. They get into our bodies and wreak havoc to it and our consciousness. They get in when we open the door to them. Some of the welcome mats are fear, attachments, emotional exchange with others who are possessed (this includes sex) and using drugs (alcohol, prescription drugs, over the counter drugs, caffeine, mushrooms, marijuana, designer and recreational drugs, etc.).

By keeping us in fear, hooked on drugs or sex, these evil beings can keep the door open for themselves and their friends to use our bodies whenever they please. Most of us are Starseeds (Ascended Masters) and are targets because our purpose or intention is to retake this planet from the evil forces that have controlled it for 10,000 years. For the starseed, possession by these beings may be chronic.

I personally have learned, as Jesus did, how to remove these beings from my body and keep from being in their effect as I have been under attack by them for many years. Now that I know who they are and what they are capable of, I can look back in retrospect and see how they effected my life in the past.

Accidents from stubbing a toe to crashing a car can be caused by these beings. Headaches and other pains of unexplained cause are their doing. They can take a small emotion and blow it way out of proportion. They can get into those around us and change their perceptions of our actions so that they react to us harshly and even violently. When Jesus was on the cross he said, "Father, forgive them for they know not what they do." What He meant was that all the people involved in his scenario were all possessed and being controlled by anti-Christs in concert for the purpose of terminating Him.

Headaches and nausea are clear signs of possession, but many possessions cause long term problems. Lack (of money, love, friends, food, jobs, etc.) can be originated by them. The evil forces invented struggle and illness and many of us have been cursed by them since we were small. Abusive parents are caused more by possessions (The parent being under possession.) than by anything else. Once this is understood, it is easy to forgive your parents. If others have abused you, see them the same as Jesus did and your Saintly forgiveness skills will reappear.

Two Thousand years ago, we didn't have the control and power over this planet that we do now. Armageddon is a war being fought primarily in the fourth and fifth dimensions. It is a star wars. The forces of the Christ have been victorious so far and the battles go on at this moment (someday it will be over and the Christ will be victorious). The power was not available two thousand years ago to depossess all those involved in Jesus' crucifixion or the scenario might have had a different outcome.

We have that power and control now. Our daily crucifixions can be halted. We need to do nothing but request from God to be depossessed. By simply saying: "God, depossess me now!" Evil beings will be removed from your bodies and dissolved.

This command can be used as often as you wish. I recommend it be used when you awake each morning, anytime you feel illness or pain, or anyplace that has dark energy. You can command it every hour to insure that you are always clear.

When you make this command, God remove these beings from you and dissolves them.

In the past, healings done by healers effected removal of evil beings from the client but nothing was done with these beings. They were free to return to your body or cause havoc and pain in some other human. In the past year, we, the forces of the Christ have given all anti-Christs the opportunity to be healed and integrated into the Light. Those who refused this and returned to their evil actions were given other opportunities. Much time has passed and it has been decided that the only way to handle these beings is by dissolving them. Understand that you take on no karma for your request. You are free. We are liberators. Dissolving just means that they are returned to merge with the Source.

Now that you have the power to clear yourself of all evil beings, you can also deal with other people and animals that become possessed. What I do is assume that everyone is possessed. As I come into close proximity with people, I ask God to remove all evil beings from them. When I go into a store, building or theater I ask that everyone in those places be cleared before I enter. This is not only a service for myself but those under possession. If any of these people do not want to part with their evil friends, it will still happen. Reading this book gives you the authority to clear all evil beings from all humans whether the human likes it or not. This authority comes from the Christ of this planet. If you chose not to do this, you can do plan B.

Plan B is only used if a possessed person confronts you. You will know if a person is possessed as they will be inappropriately hostile and abusive towards you. You must handle them as two persons: the anti-Christ and the human or the devil and the angel.

If two people approached you and one of them was hostile and abusive and the other was loving and kind, you would want to relate only to the loving and kind one. As the hostile one fired away abuses in your direction, turn to the loving one and relate with your heart. Ignore the hostile one and focus on the loving person. Soon the hostility would cease as you would be giving it no energy. All your energy would be supporting the loving being and that person would become dominant.

In the same fashion, see a possessed person as two people. Even as this person is firing away at you, identify the Christ being within and relate only to it. Ignore the anti-Christ and the hostility will fade away as the loving being blossoms into command. Give your love to this person and he/she will respond with love. The trick to doing this is seeing the person as two people and only focusing your attention on the loving being. This is part of the duality we have on this planet.

An anti-Christ gets its power to dominate a human from fear and aggression. Being loving and gentle tells others that you are not in fear and that you are not to be feared. Without this method, it might be difficult to be in your heart while under fire. Using it makes it easy to be a saint. Use it with strangers as well as those closest to you.

Just as you are now empowered to clear yourself of possession, you are also empowered to source your own love and the love from God. There are many Gods throughout creation; more than you could imagine. For the past 10,000 years our planet has been controlled by evil gods, gods that controlled us by conditional love. Gods that demanded we worship them as a condition for receiving. Now these gods are gone forever. We are in the final stages of the liberation of our planet. The Gods of the Christ require nothing and are willing to give everything unconditionally. There is no need to worship, honor, or even thank Gods of the Christ. They are beyond that. We are their children, their brothers and sisters. We are to be in our hearts, be spontaneous, creative and ask for whatever our hearts desire. God will take care of the rest. Remember: "The only way to enter the kingdom of heaven is as a little child."

Simply say: "God, I source you for my love." You will feel the love happen in your body. As with the other commands, you may say this as much as you like. You can never over do love.

Many of us have perceived "purification" as cleaning out our physical body. The truth is that the physical body is a reflection of what is happening in the emotional and mental bodies. By purifying these first, the physical body automatically purifies. It is also imperative that the emotional and mental bodies be purified before you can be brought to full ascension.

In May of 1993, there was a quantum leap in the mission to liberate and ascend the planet Earth. Many of you may have felt a kick in the butt as everyone was accelerated on their ascension paths. There have been many of these leaps since then. I cannot stress too strongly how important it is for you to begin doing these practices every day. Your ascension is vital to the liberation and ascension of the planet. The planet Earth is a key to the liberation of all of creation from the forces of evil.

Some of you may be asking who I am to be sharing this knowledge. I am not a channel, but an ascended master fully involved in this mission. The information I am sharing with you comes directly from my Godself.

Many have asked me how I know I am an ascended master. I can only share with you my own experiences. I have manifested miracles and had many spiritual experiences. This isn't necessary to prove ascension, as ascension or being an ascended master is a soul designation. Once you have ascended you are always an ascended master.

Parnelli Jones is a champion race car driver. If you saw him in a Pinto Wagon he would still be a champion. <u>We are all ascended masters</u> here to liberate planet Earth. We are using the bodies available to us. In the future, I feel we will transform these bodies, but residing in them doesn't make us any less ascended or any less masters. It is time for us to retake command of our lives and our planet. Make it so!

Ascended Master is another way of saying the human aspect of a God. Whenever one prays or communicates with "God", they are actually communicating with their own Godself. Whenever "God" gave them something or created a miracle, it was their own Godself that accomplished it. When you source God for your unconditional love and approval, you are sourcing yourself.

You are a God! It is time for you to exercise your powers as a God once again. Gods make commands and laws. Commands are temporary and laws are continuous. Write laws mandating what you want and prohibiting what you do not want. Affirmations are a form of laws.

Make a document titled: The Personal Laws of (*your name here*). Write laws for your protection, liberation, prosperity, health, relationships, etc.. Use affirmations. Here are a few sample laws I suggest you use:

1. I am the Lord, God of my realm and domain.

2. All treaties, covenants, conventions and vows between me and all Gods, entities and beings are
   hereby repealed, null, void and canceled.

Sign and date it at the bottom of the document. Keep
the laws in a safe place.

Remember to say these and the other commands in this book
repeatedly daily. Make up your own commands for whatever
temporary experiences you desire. Share this information with
others. Mail copies of this information to your friends and
colleagues on other parts of the planet. This information is
vital to all.

I undedicate myself from evil and dedicate myself to the
Christ!

I cancel all contracts between myself and all evil!

God, depossess me now!

God, I source you for my love!

CHAPTER FOURTEEN

Putting It All Together

The information in this book is fairly new to most people. It is a technology that may not have a paradigm in your consciousness in which to hold it. It is suggested that you re-read this book over a few times, highlight those parts of interest to you, take notes and practice the Five Steps of Unconditional Love and the other procedures.

This is not just a book, but a system of transformation. While you are reading this book, you are being telepathically healed. Your whole consciousness is being restructured and you are now on an accelerated path of ascension.

Now that you have all this information, what are you going to do with it? I have totally incorporated it into my life as a way of life. I now experience life as totally effortless and joyful. I am prosperous.

Practice the Five Steps of Unconditional Love and keep notes of how your life experience transforms over a period of time. Then take it one more step. Form a Five Steps of Unconditional Love study group. There are many that have already formed. You may want to inquire at your local metaphysical bookstore to see if a Joy Book study group has already been formed. Share your own transformational experiences with the group. Meet once or twice a week and read this book out loud to each other. Discuss and practice it with each other.

Remember that this is not an intellectual teaching. It is a practical teaching. It takes little effort to practice the Five Steps of Unconditional Love once you have learned them. The purpose of this book is to get people out of their heads and into their hearts. The more you are in your heart, the more joyful and prosperous you are.

Some people are so impressed with the results of the Command Subconscious Programs, that they forget the importance of the Five Steps of Unconditional Love. The holistic approach to healing and transformation is to address all aspects of our beingness: physical, spiritual, emotional and intellectual. Addressing one will effect the other three, but addressing all will accellerate healing and transformation to a much greater effect.

I know there are some great techniques in this book and you will reap great benefits from it even if you don't practice and incorporate the Five Steps of Unconditional Love into your life. Doing this will only take you so far. There is an enormous amount of power that can be restored within your being by doing the Five Steps.

Energy flows throughout our bodies naturally at a very high rate. Through suppression, judgment and fear, we have attenuated this flow to a trickle.

We create and manifest what we desire by tagging the energy flowing through our bodies with our thoughts. High energy flows create and manifest quickly. Low flows create slowly.

How energy flows through our body is how energy flows through our life. This applies to money, which is just another form of energy. Doing the abundance and prosperity Command Subconscious Programs will only take you so far. In order to open up yor money flow, you must open up your energy flows in your body.

The experience of joy and ecstasy is the result of high energy flows in the body. Love making is much more enjoyable and longer lasting when the energy flows are opened. Every organ in the body operates better when they are in high energy flow.

The bottom line is: <u>it is very important to do the Five Steps of Unconditional Love</u>. They are simple steps, but they will require some effort.

Most people were taught how to love conditionally and they practiced it for many years. In order to make the transformation to practicing unconditional love, one has to focus on practicing the Five Steps of Unconditional Love everyday. The more it is practiced and incorporated into your life, the faster it will become automatic and the more powerful and in joy you will be.

It is important for you to get all the information that this book offers. It is true that ninety percent of what you get from this book comes from God. The other ten percent is still quite important. It is rare for anyone to be able to absorb 100 percent of the information in one reading. I suggest that you re-read this book, underlining or highlighting the information that is important to you. Keep the book handy. Refer to it often.

READERS WANT TO KNOW

Since The Joy Book has been published I have received many letters. They were a mix of commendation, testimonial and inquiry. The inquiries were my source for revising this work. Every question showed me a place where more explanation or clarity was required. The following are excerpts from the letters I wrote in response to the inquiries I received.

Dear A:

The CSP's only have to be retrieved once except for certain situations. Before I proceed, I recommend you reread The Joy Book again as much can be missed the first time. This information you are seeking is in the book. For illnesses, always retrieve a new program for each new occurrence of that illness. If you intuitively feel the requirement to retrieve a program, act on your feelings spontaneously and do it. Always follow your intuition as long as it feels comfortable to you.

Goal programs you only retrieve once. As for the Friend program, it really is not a CSP. It is a command to your subconscious to make telepathic contact with those beings around you to tell them that you are their friend. It doesn't run all the time and has to be instituted whenever it is appropriate. As for the other programs, they run continuously, never stopping.

Remember that The Joy Book is a whole method of healing and empowerment. It looks like you are focusing on the CSP's and not working with the five steps of unconditional love. The CSP's will work in spite of not doing the five steps, but they will be so much more effective if one is practicing loving oneself unconditionally. All illnesses and manifestations are the results of your thoughts, actions, intentions and suppressed emotions.

Retrieving the "healthy lung program" won't necessarily cause instant healthy lungs. If the cause of a lung problem is from your thoughts, then a healing will be quite instant. If you smoke and have suppressed emotions, such as grief, being held in your lungs, then you must release and integrate those emotions to effect a healing. Stopping smoking would help also but the suppressed emotions are probably the major factor in unhealthy lungs.

I highly suggest you dive deeply into the unconditional love part of the Joy Book and make it a part of your life. Loving yourself unconditionally is one of the most powerful actions a human can take. People love you the way you love yourself. Look in the mirror and look into your eyes and say" Alan, I love and approve of you unconditionally." Do this at least four times a day, everyday. Do the five steps of unconditional love as specified in the book. It is simple but may take some effort.

In love and service to God,
Prem

Dear D:

The hurt from being dumped I have felt many times. Use this experience to cry out as much of your suppressed grief as you can. Also use it to get out your anger and rage from the past. Don't hold back with any of your emotions. We all have plenty of suppressed stuff, so don't ever think you got it all out until you are fully ascended. By integrating the emotions, (removing the judgment that they are wrong or bad, trying to avoid them, and just going for them with enthusiasm) it won't hurt or hurt as much. It takes practice, so don't expect things to happen immediately. You have years of emotions to release, go for it.

I suggest you stop using the word "need". It denotes lack and powerlessness. Just command what you want. Say: "God, the experience I want is: bla bla bla. Make it so." Be very specific and use it for every experience in your life from your sleep to your bowels to your money and love life as well as your health and getting people to you to help you.

So, remember to source yourself and God for all your love and approval and make it unconditional. Stop judging yourself and those around you. Listen to your thoughts and spoken words for judgments. Stop using words like Good, bad, right and wrong as they are the results of judgment.

People love you the way you love yourself. This is what is meant by everyone is you or a reflection of yourself. If you have stopped loving yourself, then so will everyone else. If the source of your love was removed, you must have made a big judgment about yourself to refuse yourself love. Stop punishing yourself. Spend all of your time telling yourself how much you love yourself. You don't have to do anything or work to earn worthiness or love. God gives it unconditionally. If the

Christ had just one commandment, it would be: "Love thy self unconditionally." Make it so.

In love and service to God,
    Prem

Dear S:

As far as removing old disruptive and detrimental programs and paradigms, it has been addressed. There is a process called Paradigm Shift. When requested, it will remove specific paradigms from your consciousness and replace them with beneficial paradigms. This has been incorporated into the Command subconscious Programs this past summer.

All you have to do is request a program for success and the fear paradigms are removed. Self-preservation and self destruct paradigm is removed.

As far as anger is concerned, it seems that you must feel that anger is something to get rid of from your life. You may want to reread the chapter on Integration into ecstasy. All emotions are natural and necessary. We communicate with our emotions. Take away your emotions and you take away your power. Do you want to do that?

In love and service to the Christ,
    Prem

Dear T:

I can only share with you my own experiences and what I have been told by my spirit guides. As with everything spiritual, there is usually very little physical evidence.

My experience of ascended masters is that it is a spiritual designation more than a physical one. That is, once a soul is ascended, that soul is always an ascended master no matter what body(vehicle) it is residing in. Sai Baba said that the only difference between him and everyone else is that he is God and he knows it, everyone else is God and they just don't know it. The same goes for being ascended masters.

We didn't come here to ascend. We are all ascended already. We are on a planet where the illusion is convincing enough to make us believe we are not ascended masters. I am one of the few that has seen through that illusion. Someday you will too. Someday you will discover that you are a God, so be open to that experience.

This book is one of many paths to returning to our true selves. There are other paths that are more difficult and take longer. All that is in The Joy Book I have used successfully and shared with all my students. The purpose of this book is to change mass consciousness and the life experience on the planet.

There are many evil beings, Gods, anti-christs, etc. They are all being eradicated as we speak. It is not necessary that you focus on this scenario. Just focus on yourself. They are evil because in the God game, we all chose up sides and they chose to be evil. Now the game is coming to an end throughout all creation and they are returning to the source as agreed.

In love and service to the Christ,
    Prem

Dear B:

The Command Subconscious Programs vary in effect time from person to person. My experience is that the older one is, the more deprogramming has to be done, so the longer it takes for the CSP's to attain the target goals. Children and teenagers usually experience quick results from the CSP's due to the fact that they haven't been exposed to the contrary programming for very long. The longer you believe and practice something, the more difficult it is to change that and reprogram yourself to a new experience. Persons over 50 usually have results, but they come slowly.

What accellerates the effects of the programs is the practicing of the five steps of unconditional love. Again, if one is young, it doesn't take much effort to incorporate the five steps. The longer one has been practicing conditional love, the more difficult it is for them to practice unconditional love. In both cases, the law of primacy rules. That law states that what is learned first is learned best and most difficult to change.

What dictates if someone is able to effect a change in his or her life is how much they want to change. There is a story about a guru and his disciple. As they walked along the Ganges River the disciple asked, "Master, how can I become a master like you?"

The guru led him into the water and told him to take a deep breath and hold his head under the water as long as possible. After remaining submerged for a long time, the disciple went to raise his head out of the water. The guru shoved his head back in the water before he could catch a breath and held it there while the disciple struggled.

He finally released his disciple. As he popped his head out of the water he coughed and gasped and took awhile to catch his breath. He then looked at his guru and said, "Master, why did you do that? I almost drowned."

With a slight smile, the guru replied, "The only way you will become a master is if you want it as much as you wanted that breath of air."

My personal experience has been that you must let go of all attachments and needs if you are ever to regain your powers. It doesn't mean you have to give up everything, just let go of the attachment and need of everything.

The Joy Book is devoted to the Christ. It was not created as a dating service or a way to get a job or money. These are realistic goals once you have let go of the attachment and need of these things, and they will be attainable at that time. Until then, you may have to do without, but my experience has been that you will always be taken care of. Have faith, love yourself unconditionally and devote yourself to the Christ. This can be the Christ of this planet Earth, the Christ of all creation, and/or the Christ aspect of you.

In love and service to the Christ,
Prem

SUPPORT SERVICES

There are many seminar leaders and spiritual teachers that have already integrated the teachings of The Joy Book into their curriculum. I want to thank these teachers for their support and service to God and mankind.

If you are a seminar leader or spiritual teacher, I offer my support to you. I give permission for everyone to use The Joy Book in their work. Because much of what is in this book is new, it can be confusing if taken out of context. for this reason, I recommend that students read the complete book and not excerpts. So, I prefer that people do not copy portions of The Joy Book unless they are using it for their own benefit and they own a copy of the book to refer to and read completely.

I am presently offering free healings and help to everyone unconditionally and totally confidential. To receive a healing, just send your name on a sheet of paper or by Email to me at the address or Email address below.

If you have children or others under your care or guardianship, you can request healings and help for them. Just send their names on a sheet of paper or by Email to me at the address or Email address below.

If you are a healer, teacher, doctor and want your clients, students or patients to receive help and healings from me, just send your name on a sheet of paper or by Email to me at the address or Email address below with the word HEALER or TEACHER below your name.

I do not require any further information. As with most healings, the results vary from instantaneous to a few months. The healing modality is augmentive and works to assist any other type of healing you are using. Even if you do not have any problems, it is beneficial for you to get this healing. It could only help.

Prem Raja Baba
Post Office Box 1401
Mt. Shasta, CA 96067 USA
Telephone and Fax: (530) 926-1520
Email address: joybook@inreach.com
Web pages: http://home.inreach.com/joybook/
http://home.inreach.com/joybook/healing.html
http://home.inreach.com/joybook/lawsgod.html
